Armour, Tommy.
    Tommy Armour's ABC's of golf. With illustra-
tions by Henri Arnold.   New York, Simon and
Schuster [1967]
    187p.   illus.   22cm.

    1.Golf. I.Title. II.Title: ABC's of golf.
796.352 A733a+

Tommy Armour's
ABC's of Golf

by Tommy Armour

With illustrations by Henri Arnold

SIMON AND SCHUSTER | NEW YORK

Library of Congress Catalog Card Number: 67-13453
Designed by Paula Wiener
Manufactured in the United States of America
Printed by The Murray Printing Company, Forge Village, Mass.
Bound by Book Press, Brattleboro, Vermont

Contents

Introduction   9

Advice and Attitude   17

Balance   26

Control   32

Driving   36

Experimenting   46

Footwork   50

Grip   56

Hands   66

Irons   74

Judgment   86

Knowledge   92

Lessons   97

Method   104

Nerves   107

Observing   114

Pitching and Putting   120

Quitting   132

Rhythm   136

Stance   139

Traps   147

Unity   158

Vagaries   163

Waggle and Weight   169

X-ray Your Game   175

Yips   178

Zest   184

TOMMY ARMOUR'S
ABC's of Golf

Introduction

A friend came to me in Florida and implored me to give a pal of his a lesson.

"In what?" I asked.

"In golf, of course."

"Just one lesson?"

"Well, one, anyway," my friend entreated.

"You know better than to ask me. How many times have you heard me say that a 'golf' lesson is too vague. A lesson in short or long irons, or a lesson in driving or in fairway woods, or in using the hands, or even in helping a man to help himself in his putting, or in some other element that can be fitted into the whole picture. But not one of those loose things you call a 'golf' lesson, no!"

"Please, Tommy, in the years I've known you I've

never asked you for a favor except this once. The guy and I were kids together and were in the war together. And our wives and kids are friends. He is one of the greatest fellows you'll ever meet. He's a success in everything except golf. I played with him yesterday and he's pathetic."

"Why has he waited to take a lesson until I'm around?" I asked.

"He says he's had hundreds of lessons, and I believe him. Maybe he is hopeless, Tommy. This buddy of mine hasn't been able to learn decent golf in six years, but an elephant can be taught to dance in six weeks! You've got to look at him!"

That dancing-elephant comparison won me. When I got through laughing I told my friend to bring his chum around and I'd see if I could help him.

I could. The sad case was merely another one of golf's multitude exhibits of confusion. This man hadn't stayed with one competent golf instructor long enough to learn that golf is a fundamentally simple combination of a few simple elements. He'd experimented with one instructor after another, always hoping that a miracle would hit him and that someday he would have a great game. It never seemed to have occurred to him that he might have to keep at elementary things until he'd learned them, and then the rest would happen in due course.

Learning good golf is something like learning to read: you've got to learn the alphabet first.

In their haste and hope the majority of golfers have neglected to learn the ABC's of making a shot. That is why the average of scoring is ridiculously high.

If you tried to understand this book without knowing the English alphabet, the book would be mystifying and meaningless. You would not expect that in one lucky instant there'd be a revelation from On High and reading would be easy and clear. But that's the way most golfers seem to expect good golf to be revealed to them.

Every golfer I've ever known, at some time has thought that he had found the great secret of good golf. He always believes that he has discovered some simple little thing that seems to work magic on a few shots.

The next day, the "secret" is gone.

Whatever it was, it was good while it worked. Always it was deceitfully simple. I've had it happen to me—time after time.

I have been perplexed by a persistent failure to hit a satisfactory shot, and I have tried countless things to correct the baffling fault. And let me tell you right here, out of my own experience, something that will save you many wasted hours and wasted shots. Instead of thinking about how to correct some puzzling error that you can't diagnose, do the very simple thing of trying to hit the shot in the only way that you know how to hit it properly. Then whatever the error is will be eliminated.

At one time when I couldn't get any sort of a shot that felt exactly right, I discovered that I'd been playing the ball a bit too far to the left in my stance. That is one of those unconsidered trifles that means the difference between success and failure in a golf shot.

The ordinary golfer often will play the ball too far to his left and have to fall into it or hit only the top part of it on the upswing, but you wouldn't think that a fellow who has played as much good and careful golf as I have would make that simple egregious error.

One of the first things a golfer learns in growing up out of dufferdom into playing a quite good game is never to get locked at his knees. Yet, once after winning the foremost championships of the world, I was going bad in an important competition and couldn't find out what my problem was until a friend of mine, with whom I was paired, said, "Tommy, your right knee isn't getting into shots like it usually does." There was the fault and the answer.

Very simple. Why did that, all of a sudden, happen to me? Some simple little thing went wrong. What it was I couldn't tell you then or now. The correction was simple.

I will repeat one of the most helpful statements I have ever been able to make to a golfer who asks me "What did I do wrong?" I can't tell which one of many things might have been done incorrectly or if there were a combination of faults, but I can always tell at least one simple correct and essential thing that the man or woman who was trying to make the shot did *not* do.

I pride myself on the way I use my hands. I spent a lot of money (when I was young and didn't have much to spend) playing with the great Harry Vardon, the first of the magnificent masters in manipulating a golf club, and learning from him how to handle the club and hit with the hands.

With all I've said and written about the difference between the common golfer and the expert being that the expert hits with his hands, wouldn't you think I'd always have my hands operating correctly? Yet one of the simplest and most inexcusable of mistakes was called to my attention one time by a companion professional with whom I was playing. "Your hands are coming apart at the top of the swing," he observed. And I'd been confused and wondering about complications as the possible explanation for the inadequate shots I'd been making. So, again, the problem and the answer was simplicity. There I was, a golfer who'd listened to and looked at the great Vardon as he explained why he adopted the interlocking grip that now is identified by his name. Harry Vardon himself told me that he used the interlocking grip because it enabled him to keep his hands close together.

Yet I, in cardinal sin, had let my hands get apart! When you can attain simplicity you've got good golf. Hitting the ball—the purpose of the golf swing—is rather an instinctive performance. So what you've got to do is to learn to apply the fundamentals that account for a good swing.

These fundamentals are:

- Your coupling with the club
- The correct stance and posture, with reference to the ball and to establishing a stable center of balance for the swing
- Timing (which means bringing the clubface precisely and efficiently into contact with ball)
- Footwork

When you miss attending to any of these fundamentals, you are in trouble. You may be able to get away with a little error in timing but with nothing else.

You don't have to use a lot of power in golf. The ball weighs no more than 1.62 ounces, so speed of the clubhead rather than brute muscle is the important thing in moving the ball.

Then, if golf is basically simple and doesn't demand strength, what makes the game tough? Even when you think you've got it down to essentials, it is still difficult to control consistently.

There is something about golf that seems to make a player especially susceptible to tightening up, just when freedom from tension is vitally important. I am no stranger to perfectly natural fear when in mortal peril. But then, as best I have been able to recall, I have never been as scared stiff as when I've had putts for winning championships.

My performances in the finishes of those competitions must have fooled experts. They wrote about how calm I was. The late Bernard Darwin, the eminent British golf writer, made a beautiful report of how poised and nerveless I was as I stroked my last putt of the 1931 British Open—which I won by a stroke from José Jurado. The undramatic fact is that I was virtually unconscious, and the putt must have been holed by good habit and instinct.

The lesson, if any, I got out of that and similar situations is to try to train yourself to get scared loose instead of stiff.

I see the tightening that complicates and cramps the simple performance happen almost everywhere in competition. In a fraction of a second the muscles get so rigid that any movement is awkward, and the normal, easy impulse is lost. It happens in bridge as well as in golf. Then the cards belong to the expert.

At Winged Foot Golf Club, I look out of a window that overlooks the 11th tee of the east course. By the time they've reached the 11th hole, everybody ought to be relaxed. And they all do appear to be relaxed as they take their practice swings. Then they go at the job of actually hitting the ball, and what a difference there is between the practice swing, without tension, and the swing that's going to move the clubhead 18 to 22 feet and eventually apply a square inch of clubhead against the ball at the right time!

In the variation between the practice swing and the actual swing there is much of the mystery of golf. That's the mental phase. The physical elements are much simpler and much more dependable, so that's why I have concerned myself with the simple mechanics of golf and have done rather well in that area of instruction. It's easier work than the Menningers and other authoritative psychologists and psychiatrists have to do. I've known of golfers who have gone to psychiatrists to get bad putting corrected and after the couch treatments still are poor putters. I have preferred to limit myself to the way of less effort and understandable simplicity.

I deeply believe in—and recommend to all golfers— something I read in Thoreau's *Walden.* "Our life is frittered away by detail. . . . Simplify, simplify." The perceptive Yankee said something else in *Walden* to which I long have subscribed: "It is not necessary that a man should earn his living by the sweat of his brow, unless he sweats easier than I do."

I don't believe that good golf should be an ordeal, even if you work at it for a living and certainly not if you play it for fun. Another thing I deeply believe about golf is that the intelligent mortals, whose burdens should be lightened by golf, are paradoxically those whose thinking creates, instead of eliminates, golf problems.

Hence, again, I step to the tee I long swore I would

avoid—that of golf-book writing. And I do it because, at an advanced but perennially fresh age of a golfer, I have been so frequently and profoundly convinced that the handicap of most literate golfers is that they started their schooling in golf at the high school level, without realizing that they missed kindergarten and grammar school. Without basic training in the alphabet, who's going to get passing marks in Shakespeare? And even many of those who got good basic schooling in golf have found (as, I confess, I have reminded myself) that they need refresher courses.

The wise ones admit, perhaps reluctantly, that they need to be tutored again in the simple things of golf. They find, as Plato did, about twenty-two centuries ago, "Beauty of style and harmony and grace and good rhythm depend on simplicity." That is a golf lesson from the *Republic*.

Now we'll have some more reminders from the ABC's of golf.

Advice
and
Attitude

A dvice is defined by The Rules of Golf as "any counsel or suggestion which could influence a player in determining his play, the choice of a club, or the method of making a stroke."

It is also the pseudo-instruction that the typical golfer can hardly escape getting—or giving. Because of some impulse I've never been able to understand, the majority of golfers are unable to resist the temptation to volunteer diagnosis of someone else's poor shot. It is generally made by a companion who's making just about the same percentage of bad shots as the fellow to whom he offers the free lesson.

I'll give you Exhibit A of golf's free advice: "You didn't keep your head down." The golfer who shoots anywhere from 85 to 105 probably hears that post-mortem on a bad shot several times a round. So the player will accept this observation as the gospel truth if it happens to agree with what he's been thinking in the foggy way the ordinary golfer tries to think about a bad shot, instead of devoting his mind to thinking about a good shot.

What's so costly about this free advice on keeping the head steady is that usually it isn't the primary cause of the bad shot. The basic trouble was at the other end of the player—in his footwork. Often the footwork of the average golfer is so frozen that he would break his neck if his head didn't move while he was taking a swing.

Then there's another thing that sometimes is the cause of the head coming up in the swing, and that is having it down with the chin on the chest as you address the ball. Then when you turn your shoulders, your left shoulder, instead of having room to come under your chin as it should, is going to nudge your head up.

Simple, useful advice isn't too abundant and easy to get in golf. If you are lucky enough to get it when you are starting in the game, you get the educational foundation you need to evaluate the advice you need and, perhaps, get later on.

There are two kinds of good advice in golf and unfortunately they are indiscriminately given. One type is the advice for the expert. The other is for the golfer who is playing the game as a sport and not as a business, and in this case there's a great deal of latitude for advice fitted to his qualifications and requirements.

Consider a man like Ben Hogan. Maybe he has been the best golfer of all time; at least there have been none better than Hogan. Think of the tremendous responsibility involved in each shot when Hogan was in competition at the crest of his career. Think of his background of study, practice, muscular and mental development and discipline. Hogan's is the ideal case of the great specialist in golf.

Golfing advice that would be helpful to Hogan rarely would apply to the man or woman whose objective in golf is enjoyment of the game. Such golfers might become so technically involved they'd be handicapped in hitting the ball.

The expert must know how to play, with confidence, all types of shots. The great players invariably are orthodox in most respects, with only a few movements distinctive to their own individual techniques.

When Hogan was a young professional he must have picked up bad advice somewhere. He played low, smothered hooks. No telling how many hours of experimenting, practicing and playing and how many expensive mistakes in tournaments that advice cost him before he recovered from it. He, like Vardon, Jones and other experts, has his left hand strong on the club but just strong enough for control and not so hard it cramps the whipping action of the right hand.

The experts have developed such strength in the left hand that their problem is to keep it balanced with the right hand in the connection with the club; hence they can weaken the left-hand grip a trifle by having the left thumb more toward the top of the shaft than the average player should have his left thumb.

Among bad advice given as a tip to average golfers is to have the left thumb placed on the top of the shaft in the weak position that the strong expert might find correct. That position of the left hand contributes to slicing, and the ordinary golfer usually has more than enough trouble with slices. He seldom is bothered by hooking, so he can take a chance with having his hand well over the shaft.

There are causes of slicing other than the grip. Possibly the position of the feet with relation to the ball accounts for bringing the clubface in and across the ball and giving it a slice spin even more often than the faulty grip would produce a slice. But the frequent slice certainly draws forth more free advice about changing the grip than about revising the stance. The probability is that the free advice is bad—especially if it is to place the thumb down the top of the shaft.

When you get to know variations of standard shots in the way that the playing specialists have mastered the technique of these variations, then you can change your grip from standard operating position. In the meanwhile, beware of grip advice that deviates from the conventional style of having the V's of the thumbs and forefingers of both hands pointing about to your right ear as you sole the club at address and get set for beginning your swing.

There are many good players and very few great players. Maybe you have noticed that every one of the top players today has forearms like a gorilla. Gary Player and his push-ups are a combination that developed a better control of the club than the ordinary golfer ever could get.

The use of a club by a Gary Player requires less conscious muscular effort, less tension, than a swing by an ordinary golfer. You see the strong expert wiggle a club with his hands and produce a whippy flexibility in a shaft that you could hardly bend.

That brings us to the point where needful expert advice is too seldom given and used by the ordinary player. That is in the proper fitting of clubs.

One of the reasons that I have a good reputation as an instructor is that I will not give a lesson to anyone whose clubs don't suit him—or her. I always had a few clubs of different weights and shafts handy that I could watch my pupil use in case there was the slightest doubt in my mind about the correct fit of the equipment to the player who was using it.

What's the use of my trying to give a lesson to a man who is fifty or sixty years old and has flabby muscles, if he's got clubs a young giant should be using. I'm never going to beat my brains out with the wrong clubs. Let me pass along to you what I learned after years—and what every other competent golfer has learned—you'd better get expert advice in buying clubs that fit you. The cost per shot will be a wonderful bargain.

ATTITUDE

The golfer's attitude toward the game probably costs him more strokes than ignorance.

It's a sure thing that unless you've educated yourself into the proper mood for your type of game, you'll not have the muscle tone that will enable you to play to the best of your capabilities.

Those who play golf as a profession have the business viewpoint of the game. They may be too stern and too slow and careful to please some spectators, but golf isn't primarily a spectator's game. It is the most popular participating outdoor game in the world, and the spectator phase is a comparatively late development that now is getting its most serious test.

The amateur is playing his game entirely for himself, although not entirely selfishly. A due regard for other golfers must be expressed either instinctively or because of the etiquette of the game, which is a codified sector of The Rules of the Game. If the player is of desirable character, there is no need to point out any of the fine distinctions between playing for oneself and playing with an attitude that concedes to the other fellow his right to his own enjoyment of golf. I've never seen a case of a bad-natured golfer who didn't definitely handicap himself. That goes for all classes of golfers and, I suppose, for both sexes. But what I have seen plenty of times are cases of golfers with fine golfing temperaments scoring better than they were technically qualified to do.

Walter Hagen, who certainly was one of the greatest golfers of all time, was a long way from being a technical paragon, but he had a temperament that was ideal for winning. He played dramatically and sometimes with the philosophy of Omar: "The Moving Finger writes; and, having writ,/Moves on: nor all your Piety nor Wit/Shall lure it back" and there Hagen's translation would run, "to cancel a single stroke. . . ."

Hagen never cried or cursed about a bad stroke. He seemed to regard a bad stroke as a warning to be more careful with the next shot and to play it perfectly.

Arnold Palmer is another who has a marvelous golfing temperament for competition. His technique isn't to be imitated by the golfing masses, but his capacity to bear down and hit his best shots under pressure is something to be admired and emulated in activities that are more important in the cosmic scheme than golf is.

Gene Sarazen hit a lot of magnificent shots at the right time more by temperament than ability. They used to say about Gene that, when he had to, he could play better than he knew how.

Bob Jones always seemed to me to be the nearest perfect combination of technique and temperament in golf; however, my opinion might not be endorsed by Bob, and he knows better than I (although sometimes I think that none of us may realize how our minds help or harm us at golf).

Not long ago, I was in Scotland and England and was asked to compare American and British golf. This is a delicate question to put to an American who recalls that he is a transplanted Scot. In candor I had to reply that I believed that the average British amateur enjoyed golf more than his American counterpart did for the simple reason that the typical British golfer, while desiring to play a good game, doesn't suffer from compulsion to imitate the stars and play far above his capabilities. There isn't much difference between the younger and better-qualified amateurs of either nation, except that there are about ten times more young Americans of this class than there are Britishers and that competent instruction and playing opportunities in the United States are more favorable for youngsters than in Britain.

However, in my opinion, the typical American golfer can improve his game by taking his British cousin's attitude and relaxing. Neither his career nor his life rides with a shot. He'll get more pleasure out of the game, and, by heaven, he'll play better.

The wise attitude toward golf is far more important than the ordinary golfer appreciates. You simply cannot play a fairly good golf shot while you are taut, and these days when millions of Americans are, as a friend of mine diagnoses them, "stir-crazy from concrete," the problem of unlocking nerves and muscles is one that the golfer must solve before he begins his swing. In this unlocking is one of golf's immense contributions to the pursuit of happiness.

Possibly the key to the proper attitude of the amateur toward golf was voiced by a very wealthy man who is one of golf's truly great players. He isn't a very good golfer, but in the way he enjoys golf and contributes to its enjoyment by his companions he is high in my rating.

When he is going good he gets about 100. He is a small fellow, not muscularly adept, and he never had much time in his youth to play any sport. He's had worries, too. He sold his electronics industries for millions to people who couldn't complete the deal, so he had to take the business back and restore it to high earnings.

Considering his handicaps, his 100 is what 70 would be to me. The explanation for this fellow doing as well as he does is in his enjoyable golfing temperament. He will play a shot wretchedly, and it will finish where a trick-shot artist couldn't play it, but instead of being sore and sour he will sigh and remark, "That is like one of my wife Maggie's shots. She's a wonder. She will commit a shot like that and instead of getting angry as so many do she will laugh and say, 'Well, Bill, it beats taking in washing.' "

Now there are two people who are getting a great deal out of golf. I feel that when I can tell players of their type how to cut strokes off their scores I'm repaying them for reminding me of the delights of golf.

You must learn to take a long-range and balanced view of how golf means the most to you. Try to think of the beauty of the game—how it is an escape and a refreshment for you. That actually will help you swing smoother and play better.

You can get so technical about golf that you will beat yourself. I was embarrassingly reminded of the distortion of technicalities one time at St. Andrews when I missed my drive on the first tee and 3-putted the 18th green yet went around in 71. I heard later that my caddie, one of the veterans, thinking of my initial drive and 18th-green putting, said to another old caddie, "That Armour can't play; he must have been lucky."

Sometimes I wonder if our view is broad enough as we contemplate what we might learn about golf.

Balance

Balance depends first of all on a stable foundation. A considerable percentage of high-handicap golfers are out of balance before they even begin to swing. They are generally stiff and too much on their toes.

A flat-footed stance with the knees unlocked and the behind pushed out slightly in a sitting position establishes the axis of the swing. The job is to keep that imaginary axis steady.

Balance is maintained by good timing and keeping the head still. There undoubtedly will be a tiny movement of the head, just enough to avoid stiffness, but the less movement there is the better.

Equilibrium depends on the function of structures in the middle ear. These semicircular canals are partly filled with a fluid that moves with each movement of the head. As the head moves, displaced fluid presses more on some cells than others and the impulses are transmitted to the brain. Then we know, from previous experience, what position our head has assumed.

There are other structures in the inner ear in which little calcium crystals shift as the head moves and signal the brain the position of the head in space.

Instinctively, great athletes seem to know what keeping the head steady means in hitting a ball. I used to enjoy watching Ted Williams bat. His head was steady while his legs and arms and every other part of his body was moving. The same is true of the tennis stars—men and women—I've seen in the fastest type of fast action.

There was a strange thing about Babe Didrikson when she was getting some instruction from me. She was ex-

Flat-footed stance
Knees unlocked
Slightly sitting position
Head steady

cellent at keeping her head steady in many sports, but she found keeping her head steady in golf very difficult. She was strong and craved the thrill of smashing the ball, and she probably felt that she'd have to give the shot everything to make the ball go far. The result was that she swayed all over the tee. I finally got her to keep her head steady by putting a forefinger on her brow as she was making short pitch shots. Then she learned the big idea of the still head as the hub of the swing.

A steady head is essential to good putting. Move your head the least little bit while you are stroking your putt and you lose all chance of accuracy.

The problem of balance is to swing without moving your head sideways or up and down. When your head moves sideways, you lose what should be your center of balance, and you fall into the ball instead of standing up steady and throwing your hands into the shot. When your head is bobbing, you almost certainly are going to attempt to hit the ball with your shoulders and not get your hands properly whipping the clubhead.

I can hardly emphasize too much or too often the importance of head steadiness and its accompanying good balance. This equilibrium accounts for a lot of the difference between the expert and the ordinary golfer.

I have seen some spectacular performers who were strong, nimble and in fine balance during every move they made in other games, and then were awkward and embarrassingly poor at golf for the simple reason they couldn't keep their heads steady while pivoting to hit a golf ball.

Horton Smith could keep his head almost dead still while he was making a shot, and that stability was one of the major factors in his great success as a golfer. Horton wasn't a natural athlete by any means. When a golf ball was tossed 15 to 20 feet at him he would go about catching it very awkwardly, and so seldom would he catch a ball that we stopped flipping them at him after he'd holed out long putts.

Bob Jones had the finest balance I have ever seen in golf—and that goes for all the outstanding players today. Jones never fell or staggered into a shot. A glass of water could be put on his head and a drop wouldn't splash over while he was winding up and unwinding on any shot. After the ball was hit, then his head would move very smoothly. There were no jerks in the Jones manner. He was unforgettably graceful.

Come to think of it, why should you want to move your head in making a golf swing? Head movement doesn't contribute anything to making a good shot, and the ideal swing is that which has no unnecessary details.

Harry Vardon was insistent on keeping the head steady. I took lessons from him, and since he was not talkative, what I was paying him made each word he said golden to a young amateur from Scotland.

I remember Vardon saying, "If you don't move your head you won't move your body off balance, and you've got to hit with your hands."

That was one of the most valuable golf lessons I ever have had.

I have tried to pass along this lesson by showing my pupils how the steady head, stable balance and hitting with the hands fit together in a simple picture of sound golf. I tell the pupil to put his feet together and hit a shot with a 7-iron. He's got to keep his head steady or any

Balance maintained through the full swing

part of a swing will pull him out of balance, and while he is keeping his head steady and his feet together, he's got to hit with his hands the way all expert golfers do. Usually the shots made during this demonstration are so crisp, so accurate, and so much longer than he expects that the pupil is amazed—and he learns something about the value of balance.

In good balance you make a good-looking swing; when you are out of balance your swing is grotesque and ineffective. So many times I have looked at the unlovely swings of lovely women and have lamented that they haven't learned balance. The unlovely swing of an unlovely man is even harder on the eyes, and it isn't the same thing.

Mental balance is as important as physical balance in golf. Correct thinking that goes directly to the understanding of the shot required by conditions is a beautiful asset. This balance is protection against confusion and the tendency to make the hitting of a golf ball a far more complex procedure than is necessary.

How you can get that blissful mental balance every golfer needs when shots haven't been going well, you and the good Lord will have to figure out. It's certainly one of the happiest and most valuable things a golfer can possess.

Control

Control of the shots by placing the hands in certain positions on the club grip and/or by placing the feet in certain positions with relation to the ball is fairly easy. The hard aspect of control is the tempo of the swing, and it is the essential aspect. You have to have that or you'll not get far as a golfer.

Tempo is a matter of synchronizing everything in the swing. It shouldn't be mixed up with timing, which is the term that concerns the time and place of elements during the entire action. Tempo means fitting all the elements together so that the machinery meshes smoothly, and each detail of the swing is allowed time to happen and to complete its function. For instance, the delayed hand action, that has the wrists uncocking as the hands are swung down until they're almost in the plane of the ball, is a matter of timing. That unhurried but quick-looking swing of Palmer's and the lazy-looking swing of Boros are each exhibits of masterful tempo.

You get control from good balance and from hitting within yourself. "Hitting within yourself" is one of those often-used and not too generally understood terms in golf. It simply means not to try to give the shot more power than you've got.

The average player strives to force the ball. He tries to hit with 120 per cent of his power instead of about 80 per cent—so he loses rhythm and precision. Theoretically, the ball should be hit with the clubhead traveling at the same speed for the same type of shot with the same club, but realistically there are differences in temperament, physique and conditions that subconsciously change the tempo. The experts are far more consistent in their rhythm, and that's why they have superior control. Although he has his lapses, Jack Nicklaus has about the nearest to uniform tempo of any of the stars. Dave Marr got the right rate of action when he was winning the 1965 Professional Golfers Association championship. He worked himself into that tempo, and when he achieved that physical and mental rhythm, all the shots, from the big drives to the tap-in putts, were smooth. Arnold Palmer's trouble (in those rare periods when his shots aren't coming O.K.) is due to loss of the tempo that's correct for him. Like all hard hitters, he's got to have perfect rhythm in order to have the clubface precisely placed. Mike Souchak is another strenuous golfer whose slumps are due to tempo trouble. I was with Mike at Baltusrol during a TV show, and when he wasn't happy with his shots during a warm-up, I suggested that he merely try to hit the ball a little easier. He did ease down, and he played the finest golf I've ever seen him play.

This subject of control by tempo is one of the "secrets" of good golf that the champions discovered a long time ago. When I was a lad I'd hear veteran experts say to themselves, "I'm going to hit the blooming ball so easy it will never stop going." So they'd keep their nerves under control, and with that accomplished they were able to keep the face of the club moving in the right path and at the desired speed without much strain.

To master control, you've got to have the grip that allows you to feel the clubhead. You must *know* that it is getting neither loose nor locked, but is always held so that you can instinctively guide it. Then you've got to stand and turn so that you keep the axis of your swing stable. With those fundamentals established, you can achieve the pay-off of the correct tempo. Practice hitting to some target that is comfortably within your range. Then when you've hit fifty balls within a reasonable distance of that target you can take a chance letting out a bit—but just a little, and that to show whether or not you still have dependable control.

Forget trying to get 100 per cent of your power. Even the best of them find that the odds are against them when they go for broke with their power shots. They throw themselves at the ball, and there goes accuracy. Watch Nicklaus when you get a chance, and see how he swings in beautiful rhythm right up to the critical moment when he gives the ball a terrific whip with his hands. But it's all part of the complete picture, and his arms and hands finish gracefully after the shot. Never is there the haste that might snatch him out of velvety tempo.

Driving

Driving is the easiest part of golf. The ball is teed up, and you have space 50 to 60 yards wide into which to hit. You shouldn't be under crushing or tightening tension because the drive isn't like the last shot of the hole, the putt, that determines whether you win, lose or tie.

Actually, less depends on the drive off the first tee than on any other shot in the game, so everybody should be going at the job as loosely as when they practice swings. However, I've seen first tee drives of fellows who have won major championships, and they've been pitiable performances that could be beaten by drives in a woman's Class B competition at almost any club. At my own clubs, I have watched quite good players stiffen with stage fright and forget to swing at the first tee.

Even when the average player gets warmed up, his drive is generally the high slice described as the "banana ball." Instead of throwing his hands out into the shot, he pulls them in and across the ball, resulting in a clockwise slice spin on the ball.

The drive, like every other shot in golf, is made good or bad by what happens before swinging begins. Usually there isn't adequate or reasonably intelligent preparation for the shot. The player doesn't get organized and he shoots before he is ready.

The original sin is generally in the grip. Very few players have the left hand on the club strongly enough. It should be held securely but flexibly, with the last three fingers and the heel of the hand pressing snugly against the grip. Many golfers go wrong because they've heard that the experts have the left thumb toward the top of the shaft. That's what the strong and adept fellows who play every day do to get a left-to-right shot that has a bit of a slice on the end, and which can be quite well controlled. But it is a weak position for the average player, and when you combine it with placing the back of the hand almost facing the target, there's bound to be an imbalance of the hands, and the right hand will take over long before the time when it should begin whipping the clubhead into the ball.

You'll not go wrong on the drive by applying the general idea of the left hand for control and the right hand for power. The power in the drive comes principally from the speed of the clubhead as it is in contact with the ball.

You must have the ball positioned correctly with re-

lation to the feet. With the ball teed for the drive, the correct relative position is to have the ball a bit to the right of the line extending out from the back of your left heel.

When you address the drive, your hands are about even with your crotch and slightly behind the ball.

You are going to catch the teed-up ball on the up-swing when you are driving. That explains why you play the ball a trifle ahead of your hands at address. The rest of your shots you play when the club is coming down with its leading edge getting under the ball.

The stance for the expert's drive is square, with both of his toes parallel with the direction line of the shot, or it may be a bit closed with the right foot a trifle farther back from the direction line. The closed stance facilitates more of a body turn and aids the path of the clubhead coming from inside to out and across the ball.

With his grip, the expert can finesse the drive so that he gets a slight left-to-right turn and not much roll on the finish of the shot. He wants that control of flight.

The needs of the average player are different. His drives seldom are long enough, and he rarely gets a hook. So for him I recommend the closed stance with the orthodox grip—so that he will get a big swing and can throw the clubhead fiercely into the ball and out after it.

Right here let's check on a few small but important points the average golfer overlooks.

He ought to get in the habit of teeing the ball just high enough so that about half of the ball is above the top of the driver when it is soled back of the ball. That height places the ball where the middle of the face of the driver will connect accurately. The face of a drive is lofted about 11 degrees. The loft of the 3-wood is 17 degrees. Often the long-hitting experts use the 3-wood for driving, sacrificing some distance for control. With the 3-wood, the ordinary player doesn't have trouble getting his drives into the air. He must remember that he doesn't have to tee the ball as high as when he is using a driver. Normally there would be about 10 yards difference between the driver and the 3-wood as used by the average player for tee shots—maybe a little more, maybe a little less.

Many times, the golfer who needs all the help he can get in driving handicaps himself by not selecting the correct place for teeing the ball. The tee surface might not be level and the player will tee the ball carelessly, so that it is higher or lower than the sole of his feet. The tee markers may be carelessly placed by a course workman and influence the player to take incorrect aim; so he is almost certain to hit the ball in the wrong direction even if he gets a fairly good shot.

Another common error is in placing the ball on the tee where you increase the risk of the shot. As a general rule it is wise to tee the ball on that side of the tee that is nearest trouble—out of bounds, a bunker you can reach, trees, water or bad rough. From that teed location, not only is it almost instinctive for you to aim away from trouble, but you have a wider area into which you can let your shot fly.

There are apparently minor, nevertheless important, positions of the toes at address for driving. The expert can alter the character of his shot by having his right foot at a right angle to the direction line or his toes slightly out. For the average player, the slightly toed-out position is most useful and reliable. It gives him the foundation that enables him to get the leg and body action he needs in turning around from the ball and winding up, then unwinding and swinging into the shot.

Again, in the interest of simplicity, the toes-turned-out position seems to aid the ordinary player in swinging the clubhead low, away and around the ball, instead of making the costly error of lifting the clubhead in starting the swing.

All of this comment is intended as basic training, or a refresher course in the fundamentals. I'm citing the expert deviations from primary technique as a reminder that there's no need of getting fancy with your golf unless you intend to specialize in it and make a living at it. The man or woman who is driving for fun doesn't have to worry about how Player, Nicklaus, Sanders, Palmer or the rest of the younger pro–experts hold the club but

simply has to hold it with the left hand well over the shaft
and four knuckles of the left hand showing as the clubhead is grounded behind the ball.

After you've got that elementary strong hand position,
then you organize your stance and posture with everything predicated on the relative position of the ball.

One thing the ordinary golfer can be pretty sure of
is that he won't have the ball to the right of the center
of his stance when he's got the ball teed up for a drive.
About ninety-nine times out of one hundred, however,
the ball will be nearly off his left toe. When the ball is
so far to his left like that, he has to cut in across it as
he connects. He simply cannot swing from the inside out
and hit the ball. Also, when the ball is too far to the left,
he has to fall into the shot and the ball is skied.

When you think for a minute, you realize that the
farther back between your feet the ball is, the easier it is
for you to hit it with an inside–out swing. For the teed-up
drive, be sure you have the ball between the back of the
left heel and the center line of your feet. You'll seldom
make the mistake of playing the ball too far to the right
in relation to your stance, even when your feet are close
together and you are playing short shots. For the drive,
your feet must be far enough apart to give you a firm
foundation even when your weight is shifting. Usually the
advice is to have the insides of your heels as far apart
as your shoulder tips. I've found that the tendency of the
common golfers is to have the feet just close enough
together that they cramp a full swing, rather than being too far apart. Then I'd tell them to stand with their
feet just as far apart as they'd have them if they were
trying to keep upright in a swaying and jerking bus or

suburban train, and that seemed to give them the idea. This matter of shifting the weight is something that's natural if you are set correctly at the start. All you do is swing the club around and up with your left arm as straight as an extension of the club shaft (but not as rigid). When your head is held steady, as it should be, your weight is naturally going to be a little more pronounced on your right foot than on your left. The usual estimate is that there is 60 per cent of the weight on the right foot at the top of the backswing, but efforts to come close to determining precisely this ratio of weight have only added to the confusion for the poor plagued soul who's trying to pivot. I suggest that he turn as though his right heel were the bottom bearing of the axle of his swing. That seems to give the fellow a picture of what to do and to feel.

When he's got the correct feeling of a foundation, then he can take a good turn from his hips. And when he's held his chin out a bit at address, as I've told him to do, he can smoothly and properly get his left shoulder under his chin during the backswing, and his right shoulder under as he is hitting the ball.

You always have to remember that you can turn your shoulders without turning your hips, but when you turn your hips your shoulders have to turn. For the short shots, the shoulder turn is enough, but in driving it is essential that your hips turn—and turn so much that your back practically faces the target when you are at the top of your backswing.

Something else for you to bear in mind is that if you turn your hips correctly, your leg and knee action, your shoulder turn, and the swinging of your left arm are all bound to be pretty good.

What frequently complicates driving for the average golfer is his frantic desire to hit a longer ball. He believes he is hitting it harder when he gives the job a more strenuous performance with his shoulders, but not with his hands—yet it is that pay-off of fast handwork at the critical sector that puts distance into the drive. The pattern of the average golfer in driving is an impetuous cast at the top of the swing—usually because he has lost control with his left hand and snatches at the club with his right hand.

Then when he feels that the club is coming down somewhere near the place where he should be doing a good batting job on the ball, he deludes himself that excessive bodily effort will make up for his dissipation of energy at the beginning of the downswing.

I cannot emphasize too strongly the importance of standing up to the ball and holding the club so that you will be prepared to make a fine drive. Unless you truly look like a golfer as you set yourself to drive, you have about one chance in six of hitting the sort of a drive you'd like to make. I can look at a golfer 200 yards away and, by observing the position of the hands, the ball, and the body in relation to the ball, tell you very closely what the odds are on a decent drive.

There's just one more thing I want to tell you about achieving the sort of a drive you want: Get yourself set so you won't quit as you hit the ball. When you begin to reach the hitting area of the drive, your hands are practically on the same plane as the ball, but your wrists are cocked so that the shaft is about at a right angle to your left arm—very nearly in the same relative position as at the top of the backswing. Now right here is where your right elbow is close to your ribs and about in line with your right knee; your left hand is strong and carrying the club in the direction line. Your shoulders, chest and stomach are about parallel with the direction line.

Then there is the explosion of energy. Your right hand smashes into the shot, but it doesn't overwhelm the left hand because they're working in unison. The left is doing the guiding, and the back of the left hand continues to go squarely toward the target.

Your right arm straightens so that it is just as much extended as your left arm was at the top of the backswing. Your right knee comes into the shot almost as though it were pushing your shoulders and body into the action.

And you keep your head steady!

What has been an action of "throwing the clubhead out toward right field" finishes with your right hand crossing over the left far out at the time that your arms straighten out after the ball is on its way.

At the very end of the drive, the hands are up high with the belly squarely facing the target.

Coming into the hitting area

Experimenting

Experimenting with one's game is a temptation to which almost every golfer is susceptible. I don't know of another game so marked by this tendency. In putting alone I suppose I've done about as much experimenting as all the scientists of the United States and Russia have done in trying to send men to the moon. Yet, confidentially, I have never been the world's greatest putter.

So should I pose as an authority on golf experimental work and mislead hopeful multitudes who are searching for just one little thing that will be the Big Answer?

Certainly I should, and without shame or apology, for I have made one wonderful discovery about experimenting in golf practice. What I learned was that there is a world of difference between the customary experimenting of the golfer, which only means he is hoping to catch a lucky trick in technique that may work for a while, and genuine research, which is the valid and valuable reason for experimenting. Experimenting may be merely hitting balls and hoping you will catch lightning in a bottle, but research is planned—each detail is thoughtfully organized and the results are appraised by the use of brains, eyes and muscular sense.

At my own clubs or when I go eavesdropping at golf ranges in the evenings, I see twenty players hitting balls into the wild yonder—anywhere away from the practice tee—to every one I see shooting at a definite target with a specific study in mind. Those who are just hitting anywhere are not experimenting.

When you get into a slump you will experiment with anything, and the effort may be disastrous unless it is based on fundamentally sound and simple factors, and preferably on the recommendation of an expert who knows your case.

The riskiest experimenting is done while you are playing. You may not realize it, but there are more lessons given by 90-shooters on golf courses than by professionals on lesson tees. These volunteers, who propose your experiments, give you what should be a convincing demonstration that a little knowledge is a dangerous thing. Their little knowledge almost invariably is misdirected and misapplied.

There is a friend of mine, a fellow member at Winged Foot, whose name is Sam. He is a good golfer most of the time, but what a sucker he is for suggestion all of the time!

We were in a foursome one time when Sam had bad

drives on the first and second holes. They weren't so bad that he couldn't have made up for them with one-putt greens. However, this time Sam had a partner who also is a pal of mine and a charming fellow; one of those "with malice toward none, with charity for all" volunteer-teachers. He suggested something to Sam on the third tee, something else on the fourth tee, and by the eighth tee Sam had a new grip, a new swing and no control. It took him a week to get back to his original pretty fair game.

The moral of this common case is that everybody— you and the greatest of golfers—is going to hit a bad shot now and then. That's human and it can't be helped. I have never known a fellow scoring a 64 who didn't tell me that he should have had two or three strokes less but that he missed some shots.

So missing a shot or two doesn't call for any experimenting. Simply do the few correct things you know how to do when you play your next shot, and this carefulness will usually cure what ails you. Part of the fascination and thrill of golf is the divine discontent that makes all of us eager for improvement. It has some of us trying anything once, and most of us trying everything all the time.

Let me tell you, from my own innumerable experiments, that I have learned that the best thing for me was to go back to something simple and basic that I'd known for years and in some way had neglected or lost.

These fundamental things may have to be adapted and adjusted in certain little, but effective, ways to fit the physique and temperament of the individual. They may even require fitting to the individual's golf program.

The golfer who plays almost every day, regardless of his or her physical and mental characteristics, doesn't need and can't use the mechanics that work well for the golfer who plays intermittently as a minor, though pleasant, escape and recreation.

The design for successful experimenting in golf is built from the ball up. The safest way to experiment is to bear in mind that where the ball is, and where you want the ball to go, governs everything else.

So check the placement of your feet in relation to the ball, the position of the clubface at address, the position of your hands on the club, the position of your knees and body—all in relation to the ball.

Then when you experiment with your swing, the way your grip helps or handicaps you in swinging the club, the work of your feet, knees, torso, shoulders and elbows, study and adjust deliberately—one thing at a time—until trial and error shows you what the basically correct positions, performances and feelings are for you.

Footwork

ootwork probably gets less attention in spoken and written golf instruction than any other essential of good golf technique. Generally, all you're told about it is that the left foot stays nearly flat on the ground when many of the big, strong boys wind up to hit a power shot. As a matter of fact, these specialists do get plenty of left foot action into their backswings, even though the heel doesn't come up but an inch or so. There is a lot of roll onto the inside of the left foot as the experts make a full backswing, and they have the left knee pointing to the right of the ball as they get to the top.

The average golfer would probably have too much of a strain on his back if he tried to wind up with his left heel staying on the ground. He needs to get more body turn into his long shots, so it helps him to have his left

foot work easily while retaining a good hold of the ground.

Then too, the typical golfer might be reminded that Jones, Snead and Hogan all had the left foot working easily in the backswing. The turn started from the inner edge of the left foot, and the unwinding started with the left foot coming firmly and flatly from heel to toes onto the ground—which, in a way, established the axis of the downswing.

In baseball, football, tennis, racquets and squash, bowling, basketball and swimming, instruction on good footwork is an essential to first-class over-all perform-ance. In golf, however, you might think that all you use your feet for is standing on them and walking on them as you get in and out of the golf cart to make a shot.

For many golfers, improvement begins when they learn that their feet have to feel alive and get into the shot. I've often advised students to wiggle their toes as they stand to the ball, not only to aid them in getting a feeling of secure balance, but in having them realize that their feet have to feel alive and take part in the proceedings.

Watch the feet of a very good golfer as he makes a full shot. Watch the job from the ground up as he gets going. His right knee starts toward the ball at the same time that his hands start coming down. There seems to

be a push from the ground up. As he hits the ball, his right foot is approximately at a right angle to the direction line and his shoulders are parallel to that line. Then, as he continues with his swing and allows the momentum of his hit to throw the club out, around and high, his right foot, right knee and body are squarely facing the target.

Even in the short pitch and chip shots, where the arms and hands do all the swinging and hitting that is necessary and the body figures only as the hub of the short and smooth swing, correct footwork is vital. For a demonstration of how important footwork is in these shots, have the feeling of bearing down quite emphatically on your left heel as you address the shot and never ease up on that pressure all through the shot. That will give you the axis you need for the swing that will get the leading edge of the club well under the ball. That accent on the left foot will also relieve tension elsewhere and will help you to get the simple little velvety smack that is needed.

The knee action that is controlled by footwork is another very important part of golf that isn't often mentioned. You can get away with your left knee dipping only a trifle toward the ball if the shot is to be a short one and not much body turn is required; but if you have to wind up for the shot, and it's to be anything longer than a 6-iron, your right knee had better turn so that it points to the right of the ball as you swing back and around or you simply cannot get an accurate sweeping swing that leads into a vigorous and precise hit.

The more you observe and practice, the more surely you'll learn that there is no other way of grooving the swing except in relation to knee action.

The theory of cause and effect between footwork and knee action is too confusing to worry about (at least to me), and I've tried to figure out which came first, the hen or the egg, the footwork or the knee action, for a long, long time. Finally I found out that by thinking about the right knee, and getting that to turn as it should, the right foot would take care of itself in the backswing—and my hips, body and shoulders would turn around as they should. When I learned that, I stopped worrying about the theory.

Your knees are easy to watch, and I have thought that paying a little attention to them sort of helps to keep the head steady. I've passed along that tip to pupils in various stages of proficiency who were having trouble in turning correctly, and it seems to have aided them in holding their heads steady without icy tension.

The expert can look at a player from a distance and tell by watching the player's feet and knees whether he is good or bad. If the feet are locked and dead or sluggish in action, there is only a remote chance that the shot will be much good. That goes for all shots, and it is especially true on the shot pitches where the clubhead must go toward the pin. If the right knee doesn't go toward the pin, the clubface won't travel the desired route.

Getting the right side into the shot is primarily a matter of footwork. The right knee is the signal. One of the most confusing (and utterly unnecessary) items of advice in golf instruction is to "get the left side out of the way." That is a negative, weak way of trying to tell what should be done. The constructive command is to get the right side into the shot, whereupon the left side absolutely must get out of the way unless you're Siamese twins. If you are not playing well, watch your right knee to see if it is getting into action quickly enough. If your right knee is stuck, you can't turn your body so that you will bring your arms and hands into position for making a satisfactory shot. Just this one point will make or break a shot. I recall one time when I had a lot of things to think about in playing a long approach shot, and I focused my concentration into getting my right knee to move me into hitting position. It worked! I hit my second shot to the 18th green in the last round of the 1927 National Open well enough to be in position for a rather lucky putt that tied me with Harry Cooper, and, eventually, won the championship. When you can remember a tip that straightened you out at a critical moment as long as I've remembered that time at Oakmont, then you may be sure that you've got a very good idea working for you.

It isn't easy to do the very simple thing of standing on your feet so that you can turn around without your balance wavering. It is one of those jobs that recall something Ernest Hemingway said about the hard, long work of learning the simple things. I thought when I read it years ago that it certainly applied to golf. I looked up the quotation while I was thinking about the importance of the simple job of working the right knee into the shot just about as naturally as that knee works when you are throwing a ball underhand. The Hemingway observation may protect you against getting discouraged about a lot of seemingly little things in golf instructions. "There are some things which cannot be learned quickly, and time, which is all we have, must be paid heavily for their acquiring. They are the very simplest things."

The only time you don't need live feet in golf is when you're putting. Then your feet, like your head, must be absolutely still. On all other shots you must have the feeling that you can turn smoothly without losing a bit of the stable foundation you've established.

One thing against the "flat-footed" idea is that even a slight movement in your feet keeps you mobile in the legs and body, and free in the arms. When your footwork is free there isn't much chance for your motion to be frozen anywhere else.

Grip

G ripping the club correctly is the way a golfer communicates with his tools, and "communication" seems to be the big word now in business, education, government, social climbing—everything, including how to run a zoo successfully. It is certainly a key word in golf, because if you don't "communicate" with the club, the club isn't going to think and act for itself. And when you do communicate with the club, you've got to be certain that the message isn't garbled in transmission.

You must consider your grip as a two-phase connection. One part is the mechanical union that sees to it that you will hold the club with security but will permit a required degree of flexibility in the wrists. If you are holding the club so that your wrist hinge is frozen, or even somewhat cramped, there's nothing else you can do to put power into your shot.

The other phase of the grip is the nerve message and response function. That's something we don't talk about much because this nerve phase involves signaling the subconscious for commands that are often better and quicker than conscious actions.

I've long been of the belief that much of the best golf played by experts is the result of uninhibited, instinctive performances or conditioned reflexes.

I've never dared go very far into those points. Practically all I know about conditioned reflexes is that a Russian scientist drove some poor dog crazy testing them. I am not the type to question my instincts. The primary instinct of self-preservation has done a good and lucky job for me quite a few times.

So on those points (to keep myself from complicating my own golf and that of others), I settle for the Psalmist's discovery, "I am fearfully and wonderfully made," and try to adjust myself and my fellow scholars to the wonders, if not the fears.

There is a diversity of opinion on what, physically, constitutes a good grip. There is complete agreement that the left hand has got to be in a strong position, and that means it must be somewhat on top of the club. The left-hand position is the paramount factor of the grip, but again I must remind you that the grip is a two-handed operation and the right hand has got to be so coordinated with the left (and vice versa) that the connection of player and club is a unity.

The expert uses a variety of positions of his hands on the club, depending on the type of shot he wants to play:

a left-to-right or a pronounced slice, a big hook to curve around a hazard or a slight draw with a hook at the far end of the shot, a low low, a cut shot, a push shot or a shot from a bad lie.

Those variations in hand position are for the advanced golfer. The golfer who is scoring 85 or higher had better concern himself with getting a simple, strong position for a straight ball from a normal lie. If he is ever going to get a better than 85 he'd better forget the tricky stuff alleged to come from playing specialists, and get himself a grip that will consistently stay together and whip the club precisely into the ball.

About nine times out of ten the ordinary golfer's grip trouble begins when he puts his left hand on the club. It shouldn't. If his clubs fit him all he has to do to get his left hand in the proper holding position is to sole his club flatly back of the ball with the center of the clubface lined up with the center of the ball and the shot direction line. Then, when he is standing to the ball with proper foot position and posture, and his hands are hanging down comfortably close to his body, the club itself tells how it should be gripped.

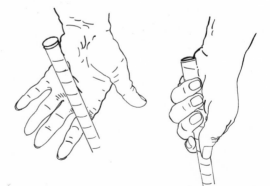

The left hand

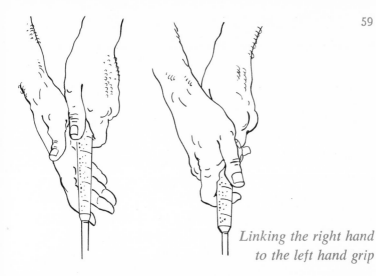

*Linking the right hand
to the left hand grip*

The shaft lies over the middle section of the hooked forefinger and runs across the root of the left little finger. Then when the fingers are curled around the grip and the back of the left hand is turned so that it rather faces the sky you have the left hand position that is correct for about 95 per cent of all golfers. Then the club should be pressed against the heel of the hand by a moderate pressure of the last three fingers of the left hand—not enough to stiffen the forearm, but about the same pressure you'd have in opening a door with the left hand. The club is slightly in the palm of the hands with that position, but the control of the club is in the finger grip. You may be sure that a great deal of the grip trouble of the average golfer is the result of having the club too far in the palms of the hands. It *must* be held with the feeling in your fingers. And when the V's of the thumbs and forefingers are not held rather snugly together, you can bet that the club is sliding far too much into the palms of the hands.

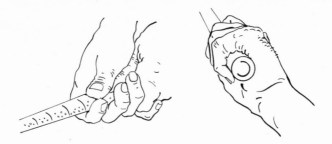

Always bear in mind when you are trying to diagnose and cure your faults, that it is the left hand that guides the club, and if your left hand weakens (which it will if the pressure of the last three fingers eases) the clubface will come in at any or all angles. What's more, the right hand, if it doesn't overpower the left as the swing starts, certainly will at the top of the swing.

So you say, "Why is Tommy talking about the left hand, while he is the fellow who told us to 'whack the hell out of the ball with the right hand'?"

The right-hand hell-whackers didn't read all of that sentence in my first book *How to Play Your Best Golf All the Time.*

> Hold the club firmly with the last three fingers of the left hand (as I told you in the chapter on the grip), let the left arm and hand act as a guide, and whack the hell out of the ball with the right hand.

A brilliant publisher, who had an equally brilliant flair for advertising, put that right-hand hell-whacking advice in a headline. It sold a lot of books and probably got a lot of chronic slicers enjoying the novelty of hooking some shots, so now to balance things I suppose I ought to urge that you hold the club to beat hell with the last three fingers of the left hand.

If you do, you should be able to swing the club around your head and anyplace else, and never loosen your hands or let your left elbow bend. Furthermore, with the last three fingers securing the club, you will be able to cock your wrists easily, as you should.

The right-hand grip gives you more latitude for adjustment according to your physical conditions. You can have the ten-fingers grip as did Francis Ouimet, Chick Evans, Cyril Tolley, Bob Rosburg, and other very good golfers. That isn't a baseball bat grip at all, although it often is called the "baseball" grip. It has the thumbs down the top right sector of the shaft and the left forefinger and right little finger close together. The baseball bat is held with the thumbs around the handle of the bat.

Or you can have the interlocking grip, which has the index finger of the left hand interlocked with the little finger of the right hand. That is the grip used by Gene Sarazen, Jack Nicklaus and a few others whose fingers are comparatively short. A very few use the interlocking grip with the left thumb on the outside and against the left forefinger. I had that grip while I was a young amateur in Scotland, but I discovered that the club dropped down in the V between my thumb and forefinger and I wasn't able to control it easily and reliably. So I finally went along with the majority of the great ones and changed to the Vardon grip, the overlapping grip named after the great Harry, who won the British Open championship six times and the U. S. Open in 1900, and taught the golfing world that you had to have fine hand action to play winning golf.

Every once in a while I hear somebody say that women, whose hands are supposed to be weak, should

The Vardon, or overlapping, grip

have the full-finger grip (or the ten-fingers or eight-fingers and thumbs grip, whatever you want to call it). I wonder if we are not getting women into thinking about grasping the club too tightly. Most players, men and women, hold the club with such a hard, tight grip that they can't possibly swing freely.

When I look at women's grips, and how they swing the club, I think the right answer for them might be in something that Lloyd Mangrum once said. Mangrum remarked that when he heard about the weakness of women in holding a golf club he thought of watching his wife whip something in a bowl with a spoon, and she showed more vigorous wrist and hand action over a sustained period than he'd been able to use in making a golf shot. Somewhere in that comment there may be the answer to one of the sweet mysteries of golf, and I suspect that the answer is primarily in the method of holding the tool.

The V of the forefinger and thumb of the right hand should point to the right shoulder tip of the average player. That's for normal, straightaway golf. A little hook is a pretty fair sign that you are getting some power into your shot, and getting action out of that right knee which moves your body into the best position for hitting.

Maybe it is strange for you to believe that for the expert, whose play puts a premium on control, the grip that encourages a hook is bad because a hook is much more difficult to control than a fade shot is.

There is nothing more exciting in golf for the average player than hitting an extraordinarily long drive, even though holing a long putt may be the pay-off.

I have played with some ordinary golfers who have hit tee shots so long I've thought the drives must have bounced on rocks. I've listened in locker rooms while those drives were boasted about, and all I can recall by way of explanation is that our heroes were standing steady, swinging loose, hitting with their hands at the right time, and throwing their hands after the shot. It is all simple, but very seldom done by the ordinary golfer.

If I could stand the strain (and if the pupil could), I would devote at least a couple of weeks to the grip in golf instruction. It takes that long to spot everything. So many things happen with the left hand that are hidden from the tutor's eyes, and he has no way of telling the feeling of the player's fingers except by experienced guessing. Teaching and learning the grip is a career— not a job. There are a few generalities to bear in mind about the grip. One is that the right-hand grip should be definitely lighter than the left-hand grip. You have to swing the club quite a way with the left hand strong and in control, and the left arm straight, before you get down to the place where your right hand fiercely smashes into the shot. Then, and not until then, does the right-hand grip firm up.

Again, and again, and again I beg of you to have those three last fingers of the left hand connecting you with the club so well that the wrists won't break until you want them to. Cock the club at the top of the swing. If you have those three fingers strongly pressing the club, your grip will be just easy enough for you to get a hand hit instead of a body lunge.

The typical right-handed golfer instinctively lacks confidence in holding the club unless he grips it very tightly with his right hand. The expert never does that. You will see the experts in tournaments moving the fingers of their right hands as they address the ball. That is to make sure that they haven't got a deadly, stiff grip of the right hand on the club. You can never hit the ball really well with a tight right-hand grip at address. When you're holding the club tightly you simply must push the shot instead of lashing the clubhead into the ball.

I must implore you to keep your hands close together. That is something else that is a "must." And how often, at critical moments, you may let your hands separate the least little fatal bit. I am reputed to be the glass of fashion and the mold of form on hand action, and it's been said that I use my hands on a golf club like Kreisler fiddled a Stradivarius. But, oh, my dear friend, how many times my hands operated carelessly! I'll never forget the time when the ball wasn't going well and I couldn't find out why until Claude Harmon said, "Tommy, your hands are coming apart at the top of your swing." And that was it! They were separating. And I was the Great Authority who had impressed on many, many pupils the sacred principle that the butt of the right thumb should press down on the left thumb in a way that joined the two hands in holy wedlock for life for the golf shot.

All the experts keep discovering something about the grip. That is why I think that in fifteen years our youngsters (boys and girls) will be so far ahead of us that we won't be able to imagine that they're the same sort of creatures. You read and hear them telling about something that you, as another expert, might have felt all along and thought that everybody must have known so you didn't mention it. For instance, Ben Hogan advised something that I can O.K. He warned against holding the club too tightly between the forefinger and thumb of the right hand, but to accent the grip of the two middle fingers of that hand. I've always thought that the "trigger grip" of the right forefinger and thumb was a marvelous thing to come into operation at the right time—and the right time was at the latest possible moment. That would be when the inner third section of the right forefinger would whip the club into the shot the way the driver of the famous twenty-mule team would remind his mule.

But this idea of mine was one of feeling rather than of positive application. Hogan accented the hold of the two middle fingers of the right hand around and on the club, and he is correct. Those fingers hook you to the club. Yet, as far as I know, no one actually spoke up and plainly said so until Hogan did. I have noticed, many times, that when I was playing my best, my grip was light on the club.

Something else I have observed is the effect of the "long" left thumb. When that thumb is "long," or extended far down the shaft, there is a tendency to allow the club to get down into the palm of the hand, but when the thumb is held close and short the action of the wrists is restricted. The best way seems to be the normal position, with the left thumb being just far enough down the shaft to have its tip even with the farthest right part of the middle finger of the right hand.

Hands

Hearing a discussion about whether the golf stroke is a swing or a hit is hearing something that may make golf useful in promoting the sale of whisky to fellows who are inclined to rejoice in controversy, but what the correct answer is I really don't know and don't care. I go along with both sides and call the stroke a swinging hit. You swing the club around and up, around and down until the time comes to hit—then HIT you instinctively do and you hit the ball with your hands.

They talk about graceful swingers, Macdonald Smith of yesteryear and Julius Boros of the modern era, and of the great girl players of yesterday—Glenna Collett, Joyce Wethered and Virginia Van Wie—as swingers. Let me

tell you that they all had swings that flowed until their
hands got almost in a vertical plane with the ball—then
there was the most dynamic whipping of the clubhead by
the hands that you'd ever want to see.

Mac Smith used heavy clubs with thick grips that he
could feel with the delicate touch of a surgeon. His ac-
celeration of clubhead travel was so smooth you'd hardly
realize that he hit the ball with such terrific speed, and
he finished so gracefully you didn't realize the explosion
of energy. His hit was like one of the heavyweight boxing
champions' blows that you have seen or have read about
as a deadly shot that "traveled only a few inches."

Regardless of everything else I say in these pages or in
the other gospel I've tried to deliver, it all narrows down
to the fact that the man or woman who can use his or her
hands can play golf. If you don't get going so that your
hands get into the shot and throw them through the shot
and out after the ball, at your best you'll be only an ordinary golfer.

Get yourself operating so that you use your hands correctly. If I can help you to do that, you have an immense
bargain in this book.

The distance of the shot depends mainly on the speed
of the clubhead. You can't argue with physics and with
velocity squared being more of a factor in energy than
the weight of the club. The driver generally has an over-
all weight of 13¼ to 13¾ ounces, so it's plain that you
must have your hands moving swiftly to get power into
your drive. What the physics formula is on the centrifugal
force of a clubhead in its big arc pulling away from the
hands, I haven't the slightest idea; but I do know for
certain that when you get your hands working so that

the clubhead feels as though it's trying to pull loose and go into orbit, you are hitting a most satisfying shot.

The only way you can transmit speed into the clubhead is with your hands. Your body and your arms move your hands into position for the hit, but unless your hands get busy in the right way, in the right place and at the right time, you won't get much of a shot.

What a beautiful thing it is to have the hands exquisitely coordinated, with the left hand controlling the position of the clubface and the right hand accelerating the club into the shot. There is the high art of golf—the hand work.

The hit begins a foot or two before the clubhead meets the ball, and it continues until well after the ball is on its way. The ordinary golfer flinches and checks his swing when the club meets the ball. He quits. But the expert can't quit. His hands simply have to keep on going—unless the shot is a punch shot that bats the leading edge of the club into the ground. That's a special shot that may be dangerous to the wrists of the fellow who doesn't know exactly how to play it.

You will hear many complex and confusing things about how and why some skinny little guy hits the ball farther than you can see, and how a fellow with an apparently short backswing knocks the ball out even with the powerhouse boys who stretch out backswings as far as they can.

But all that pseudoscientific stuff simmers down to the simple fact that the longer shots are the result of the hands making the clubhead travel faster.

When the big shots are being hit, the heads of the experts don't move. Sometimes the belly moves a little into the shot, but despite that bend the head remains steady. The head always stays back of the ball. The vertical center of the swing isn't changed.

Possibly the nearest thing to a mystery there is in the swift, long hit is the lightness of the grip that allows speeding up the hands without sacrificing security of clubhead control. The ordinary golfer doesn't seem to get that happy combination of speed and control, because he holds the club so tightly that it can't be whipped in a tigerish bite at the ball. That little, but fatal, excess of pressure restricts wrist action.

Your wrists have got to swing loosely (but not flabbily), or all you will get out of the shot is a push. You've got to have a quickening swish, a vigorous lash into the shot; a smash that sounds like a small bolt of lightning hit.

At the top of the backswing, all the good golfers have their hands under the shaft and their wrists cocked. Up there the situation is much like cocking a gun trigger for a shot; everything is getting ready. Again and again I emphasize that at the top of the swing the hands of every fine golfer stay still for an instant. There is no rushing the hand action at *any* time, but the least little bit of premature hand action at the top of the swing is fatal.

At the top of the swing, the right elbow of the expert always points down and is usually fairly close to his body. Nicklaus has his right elbow a trifle farther away from his ribs than most of them. I suspect that might have been a habit developed when he had quite a bit of puppy fat over his ribs. Kid-habits sometime stay with a fellow as he grows older.

Without exception, when the good ones start down the

right elbow comes close to the body—about in line above the right knee. That and the straight left arm are extremely important in bringing the hands into the correct hitting position. If you have any trouble keeping your right elbow down as you swing, you had better examine your grip. That may be the cause of the fault.

In bringing the hands down into hitting position, quite a few very fine golfers describe the feel in a sort of negative way. They think of it as pulling down primarily with the left hand. Chick Evans, years ago, when he was an excellent player, described the feeling as that of pulling a bell cord. That's the way Snead describes it. Confidentially, I think that all the bell cords Chick and Sam pulled Sunday mornings wouldn't disturb many sleepers. Gary Player tells of the feeling as an emphatic pull-down by the left hand. Denny Shute used to say that he felt,

AT THE TOP OF THE SWING
Secure but light grip
Right elbow pointed down
Straight left arm
Hands under shaft with
  wrists cocked

especially in swinging down for the shorter shots, as though he were trying to poke the butt end of the shaft into the ground. Shute was never long off the tee, but he was marvelously accurate at approaching. That's how he won the British Open in 1932 and the U. S. PGA in 1936 and 1937.

Once at Wannamaset he gave me a beating and a lesson I never forgot. He rolled those putts right through my heart, then punished my bleeding soul and body with fantastic putting.

The glorious trick is to get the hands just about even with the line of the ball in the downswing, while your wrists are completely cocked and the shaft of the club is at the same right angle with your straight left arm as it was at the top of the backswing.

Then, keeping your head still, explode your hands.

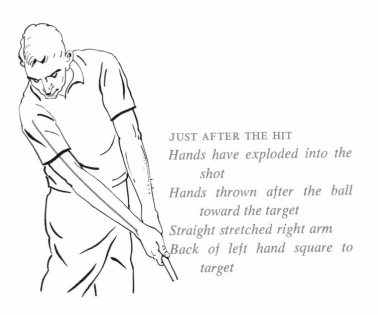

JUST AFTER THE HIT
Hands have exploded into the
shot
Hands thrown after the ball
toward the target
Straight stretched right arm
Back of left hand square to
target

Make a fierce effort to drive your hands right through the shot and out and up and around. "Feel that you're hitting it into right field" is the apt phrase that can be easily understood by American lads who were raised on baseball. With me, it's a case of throwing my hands after the ball toward the target.

At this moment of truth in the shot, your right arm straightens until it practically pulls on your shoulder. That straight, stretched right arm *after* hitting is every bit as important as the straight, extended left arm during the backswing and in the downswing when you're bringing the club to the ball and through it.

There is something else about this business of hitting with your hands, and that is the essential of keeping your left hand going through the shot. That is one of those "musts" that separate the good ones from the hackers. Keep the back of your left hand square to the target just as long as you possibly can while your head stays still, then when the head turns and your eyes follow the shot and your right hand turns over your left, you'll turn around normally. What happens then is merely a confirmation that what you've done before has been correct —or faulty.

The hacker collapses as he hits the ball. His right elbow bends and his hands swing around about waist high. But notice how high the hands of the expert are when he finishes a full shot.

A major fault of most women's golf is that they don't use their hands enough. Of course, they haven't got men's strength in their hands, but they don't use the strength that they do have, primarily because they hold the club tightly rather than properly. The correct tone of connection between player and club is one of the difficult but all-important matters. A bit too tight and your hand action is deadened; a trifle too loose and you are too sloppy to command the club and ball.

The average woman golfer has the problem of learning to hit the ball less with her body and more with her hands. That's not an easy thing to do. I have seen athletes magnificently coordinated in their other sports get into golf and be really pathetic at it, because they try to hit the ball with the body instead of the hands.

Irons

Iron play of a superior quality is perhaps the major constructive element of excellent golf. Good driving gets you in position, and the required iron shot may not present much of a problem; but any time you don't make a good iron shot there is a high probability that you have cost yourself a stroke, because it's the good iron that puts you up there for the one-putters.

There is also the probability that two or three of the four par-3 holes, which normally are features on a first-class golf course, call for iron shots from the tees. If you can't hit those irons satisfactorily, you mark down 5's where you ought to have 3's on your scorecard.

There is no deep mystery to playing irons decently. The method used by every fine player hasn't changed from the time "Old Tom" Morris played the gutty ball. You must have smooth timing and you must hit the ball *down*. Out of considerable successful experience in hitting iron shots, I can give you an observation that I know is bound to be useful to you. It is simple and reliable. Every expert instinctively, or by experience, knows about it, but I've never heard it stated as reliable basic procedure; so you can, if you wish, take it as Armour's Law of Iron Play: The *nearer* you get to the green the *more* you have to hit the ball down. That's the basic thing. Irons must be swung more upright than the woods; they're made for that sort of a path of swing. Their shafts are shorter than the woods so, naturally, the lies of the irons call for a more upright swing than the woods. The lofts of the faces range all the way from 20 degrees on most makes of 2-irons to approximately 55 degrees on sand wedges.

Wood-club lofts vary from about 11 degrees on a driver to 23 degrees (about a 3-iron loft) on a 5-wood.

With those few facts in your mind, you don't have to be a mechanical wizard to understand that the iron clubs are designed to swing down in a rather steep incline in order to get the ball up and on its way.

Very frequently the average golfer tries to scoop up the iron shot, and in so doing he completely defeats the intention of the club designer.

The position of the ball in relation to the feet varies in order to coordinate the upright swing, the club design, and the time and place of clubface contact with the ball.

Bear in mind that the lowest part of the arc of the swing has got to come under the ball. That means that

THE LONG IRONS
Feet placed normally
Ball a trifle to right of center
Weight somewhat on left foot

the placement of your feet varies from having the ball a trifle to the right of center between your feet for long irons to just ahead of a line extended from the front of the right heel for the pitch shots.

Your hands, at address, are ahead of the ball—about in line with the bottom of the arc of the planned swing.

Your feet are normal, stable, standing-distance apart for the long iron shots—with the inner edges of your heels being about as far apart as your shoulder tips.

As the desired iron shot becomes shorter, the feet come closer together, and for the pitch shots, the stance is opened a bit so that your body is slightly turned toward the hole. This narrowing of the stance is desirable because there is very little body action in these short shots. They're almost entirely "hand-made."

It is essential to have the weight emphatically on the

left foot at address for irons shots. It is imperative that the weight be kept accented there through the entire swing. The left-foot accent for the iron shots varies from the feeling that you've got about 99 per cent of your weight on your left foot when you're making the wedge shot, to about 60 per cent when you are using the 2- or 3-iron. These estimates of percentages are just guesses, of course, but they will give you the correct general idea.

I'll give you a simple point that will help you to get the needed distribution of weight for the iron shots: The farther toward the right foot the ball is, the greater the percentage of weight on the left foot.

Footwork is extremely important in playing the irons because accuracy is the objective. You've got room for straying on a lot of your wood shots, but you have to be a sharpshooter with your irons.

THE PITCH
Feet closer together
Ball opposite right heel
Weight more emphatically on
left foot

In swinging the irons back, the wedge goes almost straight back and the other clubs go a trifle more inside the direction line as the length of the shot increases. A couple of things to keep in mind: (1) Swing the club back and up with the left hand and be sure you are not lifting it with your right hand. (2) Be careful about swinging the club around too much inside, for a flat swing is nearly fatal to accuracy. There is one famous player who operates contrary to this advice. His swing for a short iron shot is so flat that I have often wondered how he gets the ball on the green, let alone near the hole. He does the trick by manipulating the club at the bottom of the swing with a peculiar hand action that the ordinary golfer couldn't imitate, and even the other experts would regard as a risky sort of juggling.

Occasionally there are unorthodox details of technique

in the games of famous players. They are able to get away with these eccentricities for a while, due to their capacity to make almost instantaneous corrective adjustments—adjustments that are perilous and should be eliminated.

The long iron shots call for an easy and a fairly full turn of the hips—maybe 75 per cent of the turn you'd take for a full wood, but not so much of a pivot that you feel you are trying to get the maximum distance out of the iron. The long irons are basically for precision—not length. If you try brute force on them, you're likely to grab the club much tighter than you should, and that's ruinous. Everything tightens including your brains, and the swing is a dead thing before it begins.

When you are playing the wedge or 8- or 9-iron not much of a hip turn is needed. Just keep your right elbow close to your ribs and in about the same plane as your right knee, and you are set for all the turn you need to bring the club to the right place for hand action. You can hit these shots a bit harder than you may think necessary, since the loft of the club gives the shot so much height that distance is lost.

Timing of the iron shots has got to be delicate. There is where that infinitesimal pause at the top of the backswing gives you the instant of truth you need to get adjusted instinctively to the velvety downswing and the whip of the hands at the bottom of the swing. You have to coordinate almost perfectly with the iron shots because the target is small and exacting.

Since your hands are ahead of the ball at address—and your left arm and the shaft of the club is about in line—there is some chance that your hands may be too far ahead of the ball at the time of impact. This may get you a slice or a shank. But the percentage is in your favor when your hands are ahead, and you are forced to whip the clubhead down and into the ball. Golf is the greatest percentage game in the world. You may forget that point when you make an unsatisfactory shot and get panicky, but you can figure it out this way: If you hit five shots that are 100 per cent O.K. and five that can be rated at only 50 per cent, your over-all percentage is 75. If I hit ten shots that are 80 per cent good, my percentage is 80 and I'll beat you.

Always be cheered (or consoled) by the fact that what makes a golfer great in this game of mortal error is not that he always hits great shots, but the modest fact that he hits fewer bad shots. Except to keep you hopeful, I would hate to tell you how many times I have half hit a shot (yes, me, the supposed Magnificent Iron-master, who now is telling you how to hit irons) and had the sublime joy of hearing the multitude scream as I walked up to see the ball almost beside the hole.

You will find plenty of men and girls who can hit wood shots nicely, but not too many of them who do well with the irons—long, medium or short. They are afraid. I used to marvel at how many average golfers obviously were scared to hit the ball the right way, but then I began to understand as I learned that golf is a game of contradictions: You throw the club to the right to get the ball to curve to the left; you pull the club into you to get the ball curving away from you; you hit the ball down to get it up; and the most maddening of all the contradictions is that when you try to lift the ball up it is sure to stay down. How many times have you seen your companions stay back on the right leg and try to scoop up a golf shot—especially when they had one of those short little efforts they wanted to toss up into the air and have fall sweetly to rest near the pin? And how many times have you been guilty of that performance?

The chip shots, which are the low running approaches, and the pitches, which are just exactly as they are labeled, are merely short iron shots. An intelligent child could learn about all there is to learn about playing them in a short time. The trouble comes from not applying what you know when the time comes for these precision shots.

My friend, Lloyd Mangrum, said that trying to tell somebody about weight shifting and the swing of playing chip shots was like trying to teach a guy how to pitch pennies. And, since it's a matter of feeling, Lloyd is so right. What's more, another of golf's contradictions is that almost everybody tries to make the simple things complex, and I'll endeavor to protect you against the temptation to get too fancy on the chips and pitches.

Fundamentally, the chip shot is a long putt that hits the green, then rolls toward the hole. When the expert plays it from 20 yards or nearer to the green, he is down in two from where he begins his chip, for he either gets within a one-putt distance of the hole or he isn't an expert. Plenty of times he will chip into the hole, as Dick Mayer did at the last hole of the 1965 New Orleans Open to the amazement of thousands who were watching at the course or on Sunday afternoon television.

One thing that separates the star from the groundlings on the chip shots is that the star selects the club that will send the ball in low trajectory onto the green. That may mean anything from a 4-iron to a 7-iron, held low on the club grip and used rather stiff-wristed like the putter. The ordinary golfer erroneously uses an 8- or 9-iron or a wedge for chips. Those clubs should be used for pitching over a bank, and not for punching a ball onto a green and rolling it up to the cup.

The chip is played from a slightly open stance, with the inner edge of the heels only four or five inches apart. The ball is played to the right of center. Weight is mainly on the left foot. Hands are slightly ahead of the clubhead, so the left arm and the shaft are approximately in line. You hit the ball on the downswing.

The chip shot is a shot which calls for touch, so play it without getting tight. And be absolutely certain to keep the club held securely with the last three fingers of your left hand so you can swing the back of the left hand toward the hole. That's your guiding element in making the chip and pitch shots (and the longer ones, too). The two middle fingers of your right hand are holding the club gently and the right forefinger and thumb are on the club delicately. They give you the sensitive feeling you need to get the required length of swing and force into the pitch. This matter of feeling is something you simply cannot deliberately command. It is an affair of instinct or subconsciousness—whatever that element is that gives you the right answer when you aren't tense and touch is allowed free rein.

Your head must be kept dead still. I say "dead" still even though it probably will move a tiny bit when you are not frozen, but the big point is that when you get in the habit of keeping your head still your body won't move out of position and ruin the precision essential to the satisfactory chip shot. Your shoulders will move smoothly but don't think of them for if you do you may be thinking of the wrong end of the shot. It is the clubhead, starting back low, then after a little downswing coming onto under and through the back of the ball, that you have to think about.

Look at the contours on the green and select the target where your chip has got to land. That landing spot, of course, determines the choice of the club, the trajectory of the ball, and the length and direction of the roll the ball will take after it lands.

Time after time I have seen ordinary players, who think that they are practicing chipping from the apron of the green, who don't get one out of five shots closer than 4 feet to the hole. Most of their approaches are more than 6 feet away from the cup when the ball finishes. If you don't hit at least four out of six of your practice approaches within 6 feet of the cup, you'd better try some other shot for a while then come back to practicing chipping and pitching, starting all over and checking up on absolutely everything: choice of club, grip, position of feet in relation to ball, aim of landing spot and roll of shot, swing, wrist action, head steadiness, touch, lie, straight left arm, right-elbow position at address and during the shot, back of left hand going squarely toward the hole, position of hands on the club grip, and, most certainly, having your weight mainly on the left foot and keeping it there all during the swing.

These delicate and highly important jobs of chipping and putting are matters of simple detail, but perfection is their sum total.

Often the average golfer disgusts himself by the way he misplays these simple little shots. He usually does it by bending his left arm, so he loses the radius of the swing, then giving the shot a jerky flip of the wrists. Give these shots enough time. Waggle the club to get the feel of the swing, then sole it behind the ball for a tiny fraction of a second so you will get the radius of the swing set. And after that there is merely a pendulum swing from the shoulders. Or, if you prefer, you can indulge yourself in anything from a small forward press to a waggle, that's O.K. Sole the club squarely back of the ball, press the hands ahead a little bit and swing back in no hurry. The almost imperceptible pause at the top of the backswing for the chip shot is a help to good timing, just as this pause is an aid and insurance in making the longer shots.

Over the years I have noticed that women players at clubs are especially inept and wasteful in making these short shots. They simply will not practice these shots enough. Improvement in the games of the girl professionals has been marked in the short-iron department. That's the reason why you are reading quite a few scores in the 60's being made in the Ladies PGA tournaments.

An obvious thing often forgotten in hitting the pitch shots is that the loft of the club kills distance, so cock your wrists plenty and take more of a backswing than you may think is needed when you're pitching a shot over a bunker onto a green. The average golfer recalls with dismay how many times he has pitched short into a trap, although he played the shot well, but not strongly enough.

Something to remember about playing pitch shots is

that as you get nearer the hole, the stance opens a bit more. You want to keep the body out of this precision shot and play it with your hands.

Always—always—always hit these short shots a descending blow, just as you are supposed to hit the longer fairway shots. The tendency of the average golfer is to fall back and try to lift a chip shot instead of keeping the weight on the left foot, staying down and allowing the club to knock the ball up in the way the club was designed to function.

One more thing about irons of all length. You may find a number of golfers who will whack the ball so far that they are even with the experts, but from there on into the hole they aren't in the same league. I remember when Jimmy Thomson was regarded as the longest hitter in the world and would go barnstorming with Harry Cooper, Lawson Little and Horton Smith in the pre-TV golf promotion tour of small towns that golf writer Charley Bartlett called "Spalding's Flying Circus." Thomson was actually the longest pro driver as far as I knew, but he came back from those junkets and told how some brawny unknown in Whistle Switch, Neb., Bear Yawn, Ind., Lost Indian, N. Mex., and other miniscule localities, outdrove him by yards.

But in all the years I've been in golf I have never, never heard of anyone who was a consistent wizard at the iron approaches—except for the genuinely great golfers.

Judgment

Judgment is that critical factor in golf which plays its part before a shot is made, and which often is every bit as important as good execution. I have known fellows who could make as good golf shots as the greatest, but who are unknown to golf fame because they failed to show at the critical moments that they knew how to play golf.

Playing fine golf is more than excellent technical execution of shots; it is exercising judgment about what sort of shot to play. That goes for every class of golfer—from the expert to the 110-shooter. I recall very few major championships through the years that weren't lost by errors in judgment, rather than by mistakes in technique.

Now, as an Elder Statesman and Old Pro, I play with everyone from the ruling luminaries and potential stars to some of the most delightful golfers you ever saw, and every day I am more impressed by the shots they all cost themselves through bad judgment. I'm sympathetic; in memory's backswing I see errors in judgment that cost me championships—and, of course, what is factual if not flattering, I see mistakes in judgment by others that gave me championships.

I read, write and listen to a lot of suggestions about "strokesavers," but when I get out on the course I am again impressed that the man or woman who shoots between par and 78 makes a couple of mistakes that are entirely errors in judgment; that the golfer who shoots in the 80's almost invariably tosses away four shots or more by not thinking golf; and the person who shoots in the 90's or higher could improve his game approximately ten strokes if he could second-guess and use his head on shots that were thoughtlessly wasted.

How much of good judgment in golf is deliberation, how much is instinct, and how much is simply the result of not being careless, I have never been able to decide, although I've thought so much about the value of judgment that I wrote a book about it. The book, *A Round of Golf with Tommy Armour,* concerned the use of judgment in playing a course. It had in it such obviously simple but often neglected essentials as teeing a drive on the side of the tee nearest to out-of-bounds, trees, tall rough, water and other perils and then hitting out into the wild and wide blue yonder "where trouble ain't."

A pleasant thing about that book was the comment

from college golf coaches who recommended it as a text book to their youngsters. They found that it helped to make fine golfers out of fine golf shot-makers. I knew how they felt. I've told about the case of Lawson Little, who won the U. S. and British National Amateur championships two consecutive years before he turned professional and won the U. S. National Open and other championships. Lawson, although you don't read much about him now in the reviews of golf's greats, was a magnificent golfer. He wasn't the finest shot-maker I ever saw, but his tactical judgment more than compensated for any defect in execution. And when he won the National Open in a play-off with Gene Sarazen, he was competing with another extraordinary competitor whose competitive zeal offset any physical deficiencies.

Unquestionably the most frequent and costliest deficiency in the judgment of the average golfer is in his selection of the club and his decision about the shot to play. The cardinal sin of the average golfer is to underclub himself, and misplay the shot by trying to force it. When in doubt about a club to use for distance, always use the longer club. You may have noticed that you are short of the hole a great many times more than you are past it.

The few times an average golfer does select too much club occur when he takes a 2- or 3-wood for a fairway shot that can't reach the green anyway, and he could play easier and with more confidence and consistency with a 4- or 5-wood. He may sacrifice a little distance (10 yards or so per higher number of club) but he gets a higher percentage of useful shots.

Television has been bad for the typical golfer's game by distorting the picture of selection of the club for the shot. I have heard golf commentators on television tell about a player taking an 8-iron for a 180-yard shot, a 5-iron for 210 yards, and other choices of clubs misleading to the fellow who isn't playing specialist. The type of shot to be played, the wind, the finesse in altering the normal loft of the club, the possibility that the expert's club differs from normal specifications, and the chance that the telecaster is guessing wrong on the club and the distance are factors entering the picture. Without considering these and other details, the mere mention of the number of the club being used is far from helpful to the ordinary golfer.

You ought to recognize what sort of a game you are capable of playing, and know that it is you and not anyone else who has to make the shot. Hence you've got to use your own judgment in playing the shot in which you have the most confidence. Confidence is a very big factor with the average golfer, and it offsets technical deficiencies many times.

There are no absolutely fixed rules for club choice. The driver is the conventional club for driving but when hitting downwind a 2-, 3- or even 4-wood can be a more useful selection. Often the experts use the 3-wood off the tee when the fairway is narrow. They figure they can control the shot better.

Time after time I have watched average golfers take a wedge or an 8- or 9-iron, and loft a shot that bumps into a rise on a green and stops far short of the hole, leaving a tricky putt over several undulations. The expert would have played a chip shot to run up and down over the bulges, and have a chance to get up to the hole.

Judgment of putts often is such a difficult problem that for the most part your best decision is to roll it for the hole. You've probably missed more putts trying to be fancy, and guess delicate borrows, than you have missed by boldly tapping a putt directly at the center of the cup.

Trying to play the fancy shot of any sort is an error in judgment for the average golfer. When he is in a bunker the thing for him to do is to get out safely, and not worry about getting the ball out so he will have an uphill putt. And when he is in the woods or in the rough, good judgment calls for the simple, sure way of getting out, without trying to play a miracle shot that has all the percentages riding against its chance of success.

In one respect golf is like chess, in which you have prescribed, advisable moves to make; you have to move the golf ball after a careful, foresighted inspection and study of the situation. Eventually you may learn one of the great "secrets" of golf—to eliminate as much thinking as possible while attending to each detail carefully as a matter of habit.

You can get into the habit of looking at the situation so the factors that influence judgment almost jump out at you. You will notice that as you get closer to the green there is a greater premium on judgment. You have to be observant and decisive and really attach the shot.

Golf is a game that requires aggressiveness. You can't "baby" any shot, from a drive to a short putt. The game is a series of attacks. The ball can't drop until it gets to the cup, and generally your last putt, if it is longer than 4 or 5 feet, ought to go past the hole if you miss.

There isn't a much sadder sight in golf than to see a fellow, with a fairly long putt to tie or win, fail to attack the hole so dismally that his putt is short.

There is another glaring exception to the average golfer's general tendency to underclub himself and so ruin the shot by forcing it. When the typical mediocre golfer gets from 80 to 50 yards from a green, he often overclubs himself and makes a half-hearted effort and quits on the shot. That's where he's likely to cost himself five or more shots every round.

The afternoon before I went to work on this material on "judgment" I played with a good companion of mine who pulls his own cart of clubs for exercise, and he played the first nine of an exacting Florida course in 37. My friend, Judge Covington, is 70 years old. He hits vigorously down at the ball. I've never seen him play it gently. He attacks and he hits with his hands instead of throwing himself violently out of balance. He knows his capabilities and from experience he has acquired the confidence in his aggressive short game that makes up for what he lacks in distance.

It's a wonderful thing to have the judgment that enables you to look at your golf in a bright and accurate light. Then you know what you can do, and because of golf's handicapping system you have a fine chance to compete on even terms with anybody. When you really know your game and play it consistently, your handicap will bring you in as the winner more times than you have to pay out.

Knowledge

Know ye that a little knowledge is a positively dangerous thing in golf. It can lead you into a lot of trouble. For instance, if you know there is a little bit of a side hill slope in the 15 inches between your ball and the cup, you will be very smart (so you believe) and play that incline with a delicate touch—and miss the putt! But when you don't know that borrow exists, you will tap the ball boldly to the center of the cup and it will fall into the hole.

In such a case a little knowledge leads you astray. Complete knowledge, born of observation, experience and thinking, teaches you that very, very rarely is there such a thing as borrow on a really short putt.

If you've been playing golf a few years you know,

from having missed a lot of tap-in's, that you have been so smart you outsmarted yourself. You are left with the rueful second guess that in those cases of very short putts ignorance would have not only been bliss, but a saved stroke.

On a golf course a fellow is exposed to an appalling amount of ignorance and is susceptible to it. This is because hope springs eternal in a golfer's breast, and when he is off his game he will grab at a straw. And the perplexing part of it all is that golf knowledge is difficult to appraise. The veteran caddies at St. Andrews, the Negro caddies at Pinehurst, who know every inch of every green like you know your face for shaving, the winos who caddie so expertly at courses in the California coastal area, all know far more about golf than they appear to know. And yet you will take advice from some fluent and personable friend in the highest tax bracket, who is a Phi Beta Kappa, and may have a very low golf IQ, because you think he knows what he's talking about.

My dear friend Bobby Cruickshank is an exceptionally intelligent golfer. He was playing in a National Open at Oakland Hills and (according to a golf writer companion of mine) seemed to be scoring at a rate that made him a championship threat until he reached the eleventh hole of the last round. He hit a perfect drive. He surveyed the situation, then asked for the help of the caddie's knowledge. The caddie suggested a club that was too long. Wee Bobby hit the ball far over the green into deep, tangled rough and before he'd holed out had taken six strokes and started the debacle that ruined his championship chances.

The writer came up as Cruickshank was walking to the next tee, and asked what Cruicky had scored on the previous hole.

"Six [and several blistering adjectives] blows!"

"Six? And on a hole I thought you'd birdie!" remarked the shocked writer who had seen the drive. "How come a six?"

"Very easily," said the amazing Cruickshank. "I have been playing golf three hundred and seventy five [exploding expletive and fiery words] years and after all that time I reach the day where I ask a five-year-old caddie what club to use."

Then Cruickshank laughed through the tears. He knew, even as you and I should, that knowledge in golf is not readily and reliably acquired at the moment when you need it.

These days there is very little excuse for ignorance in golf. There is a lot of competent instruction available. There is a great deal of information of more or less value on golf technique, and even though some of it is not suitable to every reader, it at least should stimulate thinking. And there is certainly enough talk in locker rooms, on golf courses, and on television about how to play golf. In fact there is so much that you must protect yourself by becoming an intelligent listener. Don't believe everything you hear; you have to consider the source, and if what you hear applies to you.

Carelessness and bad thinking—generally misdirected thinking—rather than lack of knowledge accounts for bad shots these days. The average golfer doesn't know how to apply the knowledge that he actually has.

There is vast room for experimentation and adjustment in the application of fundamentals in golf, for the game is highly individual. Golf technique in general resembles handwriting, which is distinctly individual, but uses the same letters as everyone else uses writing in the same language. In golf you've got the elements of grip, ball position, balance and swing, to be the measures of your personal methods. That means you've got to have very sound knowledge of golf's fundamentals to protect yourself against complications.

The most difficult task of thinking in golf is to keep the method simple. When it is simple, the correct muscle tone comes into play—neither too relaxed nor too stiff. When it is simple, it allows you to give free play to instinctive movements. I've been convinced for years that much of our trouble in making golf shots is due to our resistance to a most instinctive performance—that of using a stick to hit a small inert object on the ground.

All knowledge in golf narrows down to "hit the ball." You should not "push, scrape or spoon" the ball, according to The Rules of Golf and of mechanics. So let's have a little exercise in applying a little knowledge. You know that to hit you must chiefly use your hands. Your body and arms are used to get your hands into hitting position.

You also know that to hit a ball on the ground, you have got to hit down at it. The way the club is made will get the ball up off the ground. Hitting with your hands and hitting down are two simple basic items of golf knowledge, yet they probably are the most neglected in application.

I sat on a bench at a short par-3 water hole the day before I drafted these observations on golf knowledge, and watched two foursomes (to use the term commonly and incorrectly used). Among them they got five balls into the water by scooping the ball, or rolling it by trying to scoop it, instead of hitting it. The other three fellows merely whipped down at the ball with a minimum of body movement and a maximum of hand action, and hit balls onto the green. They didn't have to have much technical knowledge of how to hit a golf ball, but they used the little they did have. And I wish you the same good commonsense and good luck.

Now, about that parenthetical remark about "foursome." In The Rules of Golf "foursome" is defined as "a match in which two play against two, each side plays one ball." This is usually known in the United States as a "Scotch foursome," and is a feature of play by sides in the Walker Cup, Ryder Cup and Curtis Cup matches between teams of the United States and Great Britain. It isn't often used in club play in the United States. That's too bad, in a way, because the alternate shot procedure makes a player show what he knows about playing golf by hitting each shot so he makes the next one easier for his partner.

When four golfers play a round together, each playing his own ball, the correct term is "four-ball."

Lessons

Looking back, I believe that I have paid for more lessons deliberately conducted as instruction sessions than any other professional who has won major golf championships. Furthermore, like every other proficient player, I have paid in one way or another for many invaluable lessons that could be accurately described as learning experiences.

When I was a lad I paid for lessons when money was hard money and not inflated currency freely given a youngster who wanted to take a golf lesson. So, with a keen Scottish realization of what the paid lesson meant in money, I got an appreciation of the balance between teaching and learning in the process of implanting good golf into an individual. And so, by learning the pupil's position and problems, I think I became a better teacher when I reached the stage when I was qualified to translate for my own pupils what I had learned as a player.

In my mind there is a question about how much of good golf is teaching and how much is learning. I've arrived at the general conclusion that getting somebody in the frame of mind to learn is the highest achievement of golf teaching. How much good golf knowledge depends on teaching and how much on learning is, to me, one of those percentage things, such as what percentage of your weight should be on your right foot and how much on your left foot at the top of your swing. Even when they get the two feet on scales, the scale pointers don't settle the question.

The Professional Golfers Association Class A membership requirements state that five years are necessary before a fellow can become a teacher. I have as much—probably more—pride in the native and developed intelligence of my profession as any other pro golfer, but I've got to admit that I have seen fellows who have been pros for more than five years and who still weren't much smarter than some of their 90-shooting pupils about golf techniques. And I have seen pros who have been teaching as assistants or Class A professionals for only three years who were better qualified and more effective tutors than I was after five.

In the overwhelming majority of cases, the average golfer has no license to criticize the professional for tutoring deficiencies. I have had the privilege of being able to say to pupils "I cannot do a thing for you because you cannot learn." I earned that privilege years ago by telling club members that if they wanted to delude and cheat themselves that was up to them, but not to count me in as a partner on the lesson tee.

I know many more fine golf instructors than I know outstanding golf lesson-takers. And for the simple reason that I know what the teaching golf pro is up against. He is not only in the position of a kindergarten teacher, but in the very responsible job of a physician. Now think of what he'd do if he were a kindergarten teacher and had each little kid arguing with him and telling him what he thought about the problem at hand. He would knock them unconscious and have the approval of the community, including the O.K. of the parents of the lippy kids.

Or suppose that the professional were a doctor. He would listen just so long to the patient tell what was the trouble and how to cure it and then the doctor would start writing, without making much of an examination. The patient would ask, "What's the trouble, doctor?" The doctor would continue writing. "There's a lot of this going around," he would say and pass the patient along to his secretary for the bill. The pro golf instructor can't do that. He sometimes has to listen so long to so many patients he doesn't have adequate time for teaching. Let me call to your attention the salient fact that golf teaching is essentially a muscle job rather than an aural performance, and too much mouth may mean too little teaching.

Between us, the best results I've had as a teacher have been by allowing the pupil to learn physically. Often I have despaired of their learning mentally; and that has confused me because some of my pupils have been the most brilliant businessmen, financiers, social leaders, art collectors and spectacular pro sports coaches in the world, but who actually seemed not very bright in getting the simple essentials of golf.

I don't hold it against either teacher or pupil if the pupil isn't getting results from six lessons and practice. Then, for the good of both of them, they'd better change. For every hour you take a lesson you should practice intelligently for four hours. Then, after you think you have learned the lesson, give it another hour. The practice won't be a dreary affair. In business you have practiced far more than four hours on some business lesson or you wouldn't have earned enough to pay for this book. So, after you have practiced four hours, then practice another hour to make assurance doubly sure.

For years I have taught surprisingly good golf to prominent businessmen. And what has always helped them is convincing them that there is only one thing at a time to learn.

When I was making a successful career at teaching, and somebody came to me for a lesson I'd ask, "A lesson in what?"

They wouldn't say any one detail. They'd only want a lesson in golf. A lesson in the fundamentals of golf should be about a month long. So I'd ask, "How about a lesson in the short irons—or have you been told how to master them?"

After wrestling with them on that matter I'd get them started in the ABC's. For many years I've wanted to be able to get all the time I need to teach some aspiring pupil what he should know about the grip. That would take a week or more of lessons.

The lesson is only the beginning. It is the practice that

shows whether you pass the examination. When you are out on the course playing, it is too late to discover whether or not you have learned.

I often think that a lesson should consist of a half hour of instruction and a half hour of supervised practice. I, myself, got lessons at a time when all lessons were playing lessons, that combined instruction and practice. It was fun, but it wasn't the best way to learn. In any event, conditions have changed, and professionals haven't the time they might like to have for playing lessons. If you get yours, other members of the club become angry because they've been denied pro service.

The lesson tee gives you an opportunity for compact instructions. You can specialize. There are no short cuts to golf learning. You've got to learn the fundamentals. You've got to listen attentively. Don't try to tell the professional what he should tell you. Listen. If he doesn't know the right answer you'll know soon enough and be able to change to the right man.

Never ask the teacher what you are doing wrong. If you talk at all ask him what you did right—if he didn't tell you. Golf is a game of positive thinking. You will get enough free advice from inexpert amateurs on what you are doing wrong.

After you have taken golf lessons for a while, notice that the genuinely competent fellow tells you, positively, what to do. If a pro tells you what not to do, or something complicated to do, pay him off and get on your way.

I had a very entertaining and instructive experience years ago with Condé Nast, a golf enthusiast who was then publisher of *Vogue, House and Garden, Vanity*

Fair, American Golfer, and other magazines. He telephoned me one winter in Boca Raton, when it was an
exclusive private club and he was a member. He was a
good golfer, scoring in the mid-70's generally, but he'd
gone into a slump. He was one of those wise golfers
who knew the importance of a steady head. He used to
pay his caddie two dollars every time the lad saw him
guilty of lifting his head, and you may be sure that whoever caddied for Mr. Nast at Deepdale, his home club,
watched him closely. When he telephoned me he said he
was in a spell of slicing that he couldn't cure. He told me
he would pay me one thousand dollars to get him hitting
a controlled hook, and since I assured him his problem
was one that I could solve without much trouble, he in-
sisted that I wasn't regarding his situation seriously
enough. So I bet him one hundred dollars he would hook
the first ball he hit after I'd had him on the tee a few
minutes.

I won the one hundred dollars. He was an attentive
and responsive pupil.

Actors are good pupils. Bing Crosby, Bob Hope,
Danny Kaye and Jackie Gleason are excellent golf
students and golfers, not only because they have fine
poise and rhythm but also because they have the gift of
being able to imitate a model and respond well to direction.

Lawson Little was the nearest to a perfect pupil of
any I've ever had. When I first saw him as a pupil, he had
a lot of power but very little acquaintance with the finer
points of golf. He did have an extraordinary capacity for
concentration and ability to attend to detail. You could
explain to him what should be done and he wouldn't say

much. He was a listener. He wasn't graceful, but fundamentally he was as sound in technique as any golfer I ever saw, and in temperament he was a true champion. No bad shot of his upset him. He went on to the next shot and met its problem as though he were starting all over.

The professional has a touchy situation as an instructor, especially if he is at a private club with members who insist on doing the teaching during a lesson. Whatever talking there is during a golf lesson ought to be done mainly by the teacher, and that for the purpose of getting a picture of the desired performance clearly in the pupil's mind. If the pupil doesn't understand the teacher, then a question has to be asked, of course, but if there are many questions either the pupil or the teacher is wasting time.

One of the very valuable elements of a golf lesson is getting the pupil to think for himself or herself. The pro is not going to be around to tell the pupil what to do when the game is being played. Then what was learned during the lesson, and made dependable and habitual by considerable practice, pays off.

Method

M ethod is the foundation of consistency in golf. Without consistency you haven't got a chance to play well. You will make too many bad shots. When the average golfer reviews a round he has played he is sure to learn that he made a reasonably decent number of rather good shots, but his score went soaring because he made too many bad shots. Analyzing those bad shots he will discover that a substantial percentage of those were made because he didn't get organized but let fly with a vague hope that everything would tie itself together and somehow a good shot would result.

Every great golfer I ever knew had a system that was so uniform you could tell the order of his procedure after studying him for a few shots. Come to think of it, Gene

Sarazen was the exception. Gene seemed to have a different system of getting organized on almost every hole. He went through his share of preparatory detail, but in a way known only to himself. I've always considered him a "man of destiny" who could play unconventionally better than almost anyone else who played by carefully heeding accepted custom. The other fine players had a routine that got to be a habit, and I know in my case, as in theirs, this routine was insurance that they'd attend correctly in order to every detail. Sarazen was the exception that proves the rule.

You should begin to get organized as you walk up to the ball by thinking of your plan of attack—where you want the shot to go. Then the lie, the wind and your ability—especially your confidence in a club for the job —determines your selection of the club.

Now begins your method for making the shot. The first thing is to place your feet correctly in relation to the ball for the shot desired. The ball is the all-important factor, but it surprises me to see how many golfers go at the job of making a shot and pay only casual attention to the relative position of the ball.

Next in the plan of procedure is to get your grip correctly placed. Then comes the waggle. And after that the swing begins. The next element to be fitted into my routine is timing. I want to make sure I stay with every sector of the swing until it is completed, and not get in such a hurry that I neglect any detail, jam parts together, or throw the tempo of my swing out of its smooth flow.

Footwork is the final part of my method, as I have found that when I get the feeling I want in my feet, I have the correct weight distribution and balance that allows other parts of the swing to fall into proper place.

Your own method will have to be worked out to fit your individual requirements, but you just must have a system. Make it simple. The first three points I have mentioned are "musts" in that order: (1) visualizing the shot desired so you will select the correct club for the conditions; (2) placing yourself carefully and correctly in relation to the ball; and (3) getting the grip correct. Then you can have in your method the waggle or forward press (or both or neither), whichever works best for you in getting you off to a smooth start.

After you get in motion there may be matters you want to make part of your method. Some have in mind keeping the left arm straight and swinging, others want to think about turning the left knee to point to the right of the ball, somebody else wants to think about throwing his hands after the ball or keeping his head steady until his right shoulder touches his chin—or any one of a number of good tips that might be introduced into the pattern of the organized shot. But only one tip at a time can go into your method. There isn't enough time after your swing gets moving for deliberately thinking and doing two or more things.

Nerves

Nervousness about a golf shot comes from uncertainty. Nobody ever is nervous about a practice swing or a practice putt, hence these strokes usually are well made. To the 100-shooter, playing entirely for recreation, tight or shaky nerves ought not to be a factor in any golf situation. But this logic doesn't work, for when this just-for-fun golfer gets where he needs a loose, easy shot to get across a bunker or a pond he gets uncertain about it. Instead of having any definite way of playing the shot his uncertainty takes over his nerves, and he knocks the ball exactly where he does not want it to go.

I've only known of one ordinary golfer who was able to fool his nerves, but not for long. This friend had very good luck with his critical putts by pretending he had missed his first try, the one that really counted, and now was only second-guessing with nothing riding on the outcome of the putt. He holed a lot of them by pretending they didn't mean anything. That shows you how nutty golfers can get.

The expert who plays golf for a living or for glory learns that golf is a game of extreme delicacy and that nerves are part of the game. He has his early years of big time competition in which he is confident to the point of cockiness, and nerves don't disturb him. He doesn't know so many important putts can be missed. Then, after some years, his decline begins. The decline in not a matter of diminishing ability, physical incapacity or lack of knowledge. He is, in a way, punch-drunk, as the years of pressure have beaten him down so he cannot function under stress as he did when he was younger.

I think I quit when I was at the crest of my ability. During the Canadian Open of 1934, I told my wife that this was the last big competition I'd take seriously. It was getting so that I couldn't master my nerves.

One of the most punishing things about top class golf competition is imagination. You imagine what could happen instead of what should happen. Then you've had it!

Unfortunately the short game is where the nerves first jump out of the experienced contestant's skin. Short putts that you never missed and never thought about missing when you were fresh in competition become frightful. They couldn't be more dangerous if they were mined. Fellows who have been decorated for cool bravery in battle sweat and shake in fear as they look at a 3-foot putt.

Ben Hogan, surely an immortal of golf over a long career, developed one of the worst cases of golf-battered nerves I have seen. I watched him at Winged Foot during the National Open of 1959 play from tee to green as nearly perfectly as a human could. Then on the green he putted so awfully that he moved strong men to tears. He could hardly draw the putter back or swing it toward the hole. As late as the PGA championships of 1964 and 1965, and the Masters of 1966, Hogan would have won had he been able to putt like the winners. Looking at Hogan during latter-year championships, you'd think him nerveless, until he bent over to putt. Then the fellow who's been through it knew the Hogan nerves were holding him helpless in hell.

Excellent golfers who, you'd think, have shakeproof temperaments often are fighting nerves. For a while some of the tournament circuit regulars took so many tranquilizer pills their companions said they rattled like dice boxes, but the tranquilizers didn't quiet the short game nerves. Some take a deep breath and hold it as they try to keep their nerves under control. Others go early to bed, whether or not they sleep, and some even try to miss sleep and get so tired they hope they won't know they've got nerves. Cigarettes, alligator steaks, aspirin, Alka Seltzer and heaven knows what else are among the placebos professional golfers take to lull the nerves.

A number of the old school of stars used to regard whisky as a sovereign remedy for nerves. They took the treatment in the manner that W. C. Fields mentioned in one of his pictures: "I took a cup of booze to quiet my nerves. I repeated the treatment until my nerves got so quiet I couldn't move." Other earlier champions never touched whisky, and they suffered from nerves just the same as the thirsty fellows.

Walter Hagen was a great one for shifting the mental scenery so what could have been a tragic crisis became a situation of confident showmanship. There is an item of folklore about Hagen holing the winning putt at Hoylake in the 1924 British Open to beat Ernest Whitcombe by a stroke. Hagen was asked if he hadn't been nervous about that 5-foot putt. Walter replied (so the story goes), "No. Why should I have been? I knew that if I missed I could beat him in the play-off." That remark was characteristic of Hagen. He had temperament that was as near pressure-proof in the clutches as any golfer I've ever seen.

Maybe you can dramatize yourself to yourself so you'll lessen the tension. Once in a while I've been able to do it. In the days when we used to have those head-to-head match play contests in the PGA championship I could control my own tendency to tension by thinking of the other fellow being more worried than I was.

In this era Jack Nicklaus is at the stage where he should have less tension than the opposition. He is young, able and conquering. When anybody goes into a play-off against Nicklaus it surely isn't Nicklaus who has to tighten with uncertainty. However, again, the theory of the causes of nervousness and tension is anybody's guess, and the case might be that the player with the better record has much to lose and little to gain in prestige by defeating some fellow who isn't generally regarded as being in the same class with the Great One. That accounts for the Great One getting knocked off now and then by nerves sneaking in.

Nervousness seems to be particularly severe in golf. One reason is that it's an individual game, and you can't depend on or blame teammates. Also, because it has such frequent intervals of physical immobility, one's mentality is jumping around doing mischievous tricks.

Since nerves are here to stay, the only thing we can do is to devise intellectual and physical disciplines to control them. We don't want to eliminate tension and get saggy, sloppy and weak in our positions and actions. Muscle tone that generates and releases energy is a phase essential to good golf. The golfer's problem is to make tension a helpful tool and not allow it to be a handicap.

One of the many strange things about nerves in golf is the matter of betting. Some golfers I've met actually seem to be able to control themselves better when they have a big wager on a shot. Others—and some of them are rich men and liberal spenders—tighten stiff on a critical shot in a dollar Nassau. Theoretically golf is the same sort of competition whether it's a dime a hole, or a $250,000 Open tournament. Money doesn't make the shot. You can't possibly buy a shot.

Possibly the soundest philosophy is that of the veteran Bill Langford, who was one of the earlier eastern intercollegiate stars and who became an excellent golf course architect. Bill maintains that a man never should bet enough on a golf game to make the bet more important than the golf.

Whatever the origin of nervousness, there is a definite pattern in its course. First, under tension, the grip tightens, then the forearms, the shoulders, the body and legs stiffen in a chain reaction, then finally the brain tightens and you are hopeless. Sheer luck and animal instinct gets you hitting the ball in a wild way.

The only generally certain and simple way of protecting yourself is to start with your grip fairly loose. Just the gentle pressure of the last two or three fingers of your left hand with possibly the feeling of pressure accented on the tips of those fingers as they curl around the club, is the only definite, localized sensation of tightness you need. And that doesn't need to be tight to keep the club from turning, or to avoid flinching as you hit. The rest of the grip is mainly a matter of placement of the hands together and on the shaft. When the fingers and hands are correctly located in the grip, there is an instinctive firming of the connection as the ball is being hit.

Your right hand goes along as a passenger during the greater part of the swing. It's just enough of a helper to ease the left hand's vital job of controlling the club. And when I say "left hand" I mean mainly the last three fingers of the left hand pushing the club grip into the heel of that hand just firmly enough to provide a secure connection that won't allow the club to loosen anywhere during the swing. Remember, this is especially true at the top where the grip must have, in addition to security and control, flexibility for cocking the wrists.

The place where you should be sure to have a relaxed but not loose grip is at the top of the swing, not when you begin swinging. Many golfers hold the club very loosely when they are waggling the club or at the start of the swing, but the first thing they do going back is to tighten the hold. Then when they get to the top they are frozen and have to jerk loose. That's the way timing is ruined. And that's where most of the "look-ups" begin.

Nothing eases nerves like hitting a few good shots. Maybe you hit a poor drive off the first tee. Then you feel that you've got to make up for lost distance and grimly determine to muscle the next shot. By the time you have tried everything else and in defeat and disgust practically quit trying, you become loose enough to put life into the shot. Unfortunately, the average golfer doesn't then realize that he has demonstrated that the salvation of his game lies in his liberation from excessive tension.

You probably have heard playing companions ask, in delighted surprise, "What did I do then?" after they've made a very good shot. The right answer, about eight times out of ten is, "You hit the ball without tightening on your swing."

There's another experience common to the ordinary golfer that sometimes happily mystifies him. He gets into the rough and then, with a death-like grip on his club, tries to power the shot out and gets it only a few yards. But, at least he does get the ball nearer to the fairway, so he eases up on the second shot, and when he is not handicapped by tension the lively easy swing rifles the ball up out of the tall grass and on its way.

Truly great golfers are aware that tension is a peril that spares no golfer. The great ones miss shots when they tighten up and that knowledge of danger generally gives them enough of a warning to conquer tension by whatever ways temperament and experience have taught. When the average golfer asks me what to do when he gets nervous about making a shot, all I can tell him is "nothing." Maybe in some fortunate way he can imagine that he doesn't know what he's up against, and that he hasn't got any nerves or imagination or brains.

Observing

Offhand I'd say that there are at least a half dozen fine shot-makers in pro golf who aren't nearly as high as they should be in the financial scoring for the plain reason that they do not know how to play golf. Their judgment in playing shots is faulty and expensive, because they have not learned how to look at a course and see all there is to know. They haven't acquired the art and science of observing, and what gets them in nearly every tournament is an unexpected development, something like the ditch at Waterloo that changed history.

Jack Nicklaus is one of the keenest observers and readers of a golf course I've ever seen. He has genius of the Hogan order in this phase of golf. He sees everything to make the shot *and the next one* as easy as his brains can make them. The fellow who can read a course and knows his game has the percentage going with him. Even when he misses a shot he "misses it good," and he doesn't often lose a shot irreparably.

Ralph Guldahl, in winning two National Opens on two different types of courses, Oakland Hills at Detroit and Cherry Hills at Denver, saw and played the shots that fitted his type of a game to the particular course. Cary Middlecoff, who won National Opens at Medinah near Chicago and at Oak Hills at Rochester, read courses in a way that demanded a precise shot as the answer. If the shot didn't come off exactly, he was risking a lot of trouble. Sam Snead seems to have had the misfortune of hitting to spots where he was in bad trouble if the shots weren't exactly right. And that is the story of a most magnificent shot-maker's failure to ever win the Open.

I have seen quite a number of wily senior golfers keenly observe course architecture, turf, weather conditions and other factors in determining their tactics for playing a hole. Time after time I've seen their one-putt pars and birdies beat competitors who were 50 yards longer off the tee, and 25 to 35 yards longer with fairway shots. They do well by heeding the old saying "In golf it's not how, but how many."

The average golfer looks without seeing when he is playing a course. I'm often inclined to believe that the fellow hasn't the slightest realization that he is playing a course designed to make him think, and play with his brains as well as with his body.

The course that is a genuine work of art is one that tempts, rewards, punishes, distresses and delights and, in its own way, sets the stage for the golfer's Pilgrim's Progress.

If a hole is sound architecturally it can be played correctly by mind as well as by the muscle of the slam-bang strong youths who play from the back markers on tees that are 100 yards long. But you've got to be keenly and completely observant if you are to outthink the course, and save strokes that way.

When you look at a shot you should bear in mind that the word "observe" means "to notice or perceive (something), to pay special attention to, to examine scientifically." Then you will carefully notice and fit into the plan of the shot such things as: the nature of the lie; the wind between you and the green and how the flag indicates the wind is at the green; what risks to avoid in bunkers, trees, out-of-bounds, water, ditches, etc; how the slope of terrain will help or handicap you; where the pin is placed and how the contour of the green may deflect your ball toward the hole or toward a hazard where the tee markers are placed; and other details that will occur to you as you begin to get the habit of vigilance in playing a course.

Tee markers are often so carelessly placed that they give the unobservant player misleading aim for his shot. They may have him playing where his feet aren't on level turf.

In observing the situation you should consider what sort of shot your opponent has, and what the competitive situation is. Especially in putting you may be able to learn something useful from him if you observe carefully.

You ought to check distance on your own course from landmarks out from the green. Many courses have markers along fairways and 150 yards out from the centers of greens, but you've got to know a lot more than that if you are going to play your shots so that your eyes and brain help you. Note on your scorecard the significant distance of bunkers from tees and from greens, the useful distances of conspicuous trees, posts, fences, ponds, creeks, bridges, paths and buildings—anything that might be helpful to you in estimating distances. Although there's a lot of difference between a professional playing for a livelihood and a man, woman or youngster playing golf sheerly for the fun of it, the matter of observing every aspect of the problem of the shot is interesting as well as important for any golfer.

Observing the contour and the grain of the greens is only one way in which you can get a true mental picture of the putt you have to make. When you've sharply visualized the putt you can resist the temptation to move your head and look at it again. You already know with your mind's eye how the putt looks if you have observed well, and have selected an aiming point. It is probable that the best advice that can be given any average golfer (and maybe the low handicap ones) is to tell him to take a good look at the contours that determine the line to the hole, and make an unscared guess at the speed of the green and the necessary "touch" to keep the ball on the line. And then get on with it.

A lot of the stuff you read about tapping the putt with the toe of the putter to hook it so it will stay on the line of a putt that curves uphill, and the rest of that stuff that calls for carrying a computer in your pocket, is too fancy for me. Maybe there are fellows who can observe the line of a putt with a couple of borrows in it so exactly, and, what's more, play it so precisely, that the ball will follow a patch like a mountain road—but I've never met any of them.

When I was reading greens best, about all I could observe clearly was that if the line looked shiny the grain of the grass was running toward the hole, so I should stroke the putt a trifle easier. If the hole itself looked as though it were set on a slant, I had to roll the ball toward the high side and hope and listen.

That dependable generality about greens sloping away from mountains and toward the ocean should be something that the most obtuse of us could and would observe, but many times many of us have not seen its truth, and that blindness has been to our regret.

There are numerous delicate borrows near the hole that we may not observe, but that's probably just as well because then we don't get dainty and "baby" the putt in such a way that it won't keep any line to the cup. If we make mistakes in observing green contours it is better for us to guess wrong on the high side, so the putt may have a chance to tumble in. But, come to think of it, Joe Kirkwood missed winning a British Open by having putts miss on the low side (the "amateur side" of the hole) although you'd think that the greatest of all trick shot artists could correctly read every little nicety of a green.

Sometimes I think that the typical club golfer has to be more "expert" than the expert in reading the line of putts ranging from 2 to 7 feet, since the cup placement at clubs frequently is at any spot at all where the fancy of the man with the hole-digger happens to dwell. If contestants in a National Open championship had to putt to cups on the sidehill locations they often are at private clubs, there would be agonized wails of protest. At the pay-for-play courses cup placement generally is fair, as the greens are fairly flat, and good operation of such courses calls for getting the players off the green as soon as possible.

Another practical point about observing golf greens is that modern turf management has virtually eliminated nap or grain of greens so you don't have to allow for that factor in inspecting the line of your putt.

Pitching
and
Putting

Prepare now for the most delicate, difficult and important part of the game. In this category are the precision shots from 50 yards and nearer, that roll up to the cup to either write off mistakes you might have made since you hit the ball off the tee, or add sorry little strokes that mean the difference between a decent score and one you don't want mentioned aloud.

It is the short game that separates the champions from the losers in every class from A to Z. Pitching by experts is beautiful to watch. When done by the average golfer it is often hideous and sad to behold. The pitch, whether it is deftly lobbed and drops with a bite and a backswing, or curves lower in the air and turns toward the target, is a shot of definite positions in preparation, and delicate feel and rhythm in execution.

The chip shot—the short approach from off the green that hits and runs after a low trajectory—is practically a putt with a 4- to a 7-iron, depending on what distance the ball is to go in the air, where it is to land on the green, and how far you want it to roll. Apply whatever you know about putting to pitching, with a slightly lofted club and a shorter grip, and you've got it made. There are almost as many allowances for variations in chipping technique as there are in putting methods, with only the essentials of a steady head and keeping the clubface squarely across the direction line to keep in mind.

But those lofted pitch shots don't permit much deviation from the conventional. You've got to do them exactly right or else. Fortunately it really isn't much of a trick to play the pitch shots well, as the method of all the fine golfers is uniform. They get the right "touch" by hours of practice. Show me the average golfer who gives much time to practicing pitch shots and that golfer is going to be much better than average before many weeks have passed.

The method of all the excellent golfers when they're playing a pitch shot is as follows:

- Feet close together; heels almost touching
- Slightly open stance with the weight on left foot
- Hands in front of the ball
- An upright swing

Let's go into a bit of explaining as to why these four points are essential.

The relationship of the left arm
to the club shaft is indicated here

The feet close together helps you to stand still. The pitch shot isn't a long swing. It is a short job with a crisp hit with the hands. But remember one thing about this short swing in pitching: Make the swing a little longer than you may think necessary because the loft of the club is going to kill some of the distance you want.

The slightly open stance helps you to swing more upright. The upright swing is an absolute "must" on pitch shots. You cannot possibly get away with a flat, roundhouse swing. And by an upright swing I mean "swing" as well as "upright." Swing the club away low to the ground for a few inches and swing it with your left arm straight so you will resist the temptation to lift the club with your right hand and hack down behind the ball or top it. You have got to get the leading edge of the club well underneath the ball so the "sweet spot" of the club-

THE ADDRESS ON PITCH SHOTS
Hands in front of ball
Weight on left foot
Feet close together
Slightly open stance

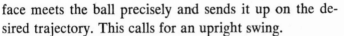

face meets the ball precisely and sends it up on the de-sired trajectory. This calls for an upright swing.

Having the hands in front of the ball at address helps you to keep your weight forward—mainly on your left foot—all during the shot and in that way gets you hitting down as you should.

I recommend a slightly firmer grip with the last three fingers of the left hand when you are making the pitches. You must have a sharp contact with these shots. You can't get by with anything whippy or flabby. The shot has got to be decisive in every way.

You should have a short follow-through with the pitch shot. That will assure that you won't quit on the shot but definitely hit it to where it ought to go.

That seems like a lot of detail for just one little short shot, and even this presumes that you are in good balance so you won't move your head and take your entire physical organization out of alignment. But if you slight any of these three simple points in preparing for the pitch shot, I hope you will be sure not to forget to have your hands in front of the ball at address, and the shaft of the club and your left arm in line, for when you attend to just that one thing the other details pretty much fall into the correct arrangement.

Most common of the errors in making the pitch shots is that of having the weight on the right foot, instead of on the left. That mistake is made by some of the good ones at times, and why that mortal error occurs nobody has been able to explain. Anyone who is experienced in golf knows that keeping weight accented on the left foot is imperative. I'll never forget a tragic exhibition of this error as far back as the 1923 USGA Women's Amateur championship at the Westchester–Biltmore Country Club. Alexe Stirling and Edith Cummings were playing in the finals. Miss Stirling had been medalist in the qualifying rounds of the championship. She had won the title in 1916, and after the war, when the championship was renewed in 1919, won again in 1920 and was runner-up in 1921. She was one of our great players. Miss Cummings was one of the finest golfers in the Midwest. When Miss Stirling got 40 to 50 yards from the pin on three holes, she hit her pitches with her weight mainly on the right foot and, of course, topped them or scuffed them in a shockingly incompetent manner, and lost those three holes, although normally she would have pitched near enough to have good chances for one-putting. She lost the championship to Miss Cummings, 3 and 2.

It is very easy to make the mistake of using too much

wrist at the wrong time on the pitch shots. The average golfer tries to hit the short pitches by flicking his wrists instead of swinging the club back a little, then cocking his wrists, taking that almost imperceptible pause at the top of the backswing, and uncocking his wrists at the last possible moment when his arms swing the hands down until they're in the same plane as the ball, or even a wee bit ahead of it.

There is a most important point that you can take as a law of good golf—the nearer the hole the steadier the head has got to be in playing the shot. You can have a tiny bit of head movement when you're pitching the ball to the green—just enough to keep your body from being tight but not enough so you risk altering the axis of your swing. The shorter your shot the greater is the risk of error in moving your head.

Selection of the club for the short pitch shot is important. The average golfer tries to get spin on a pitch and back up the ball after it hits the green. So almost invariably he uses a pitching wedge and attempts to cut under the ball and play a cutely manipulated shot, instead of playing a simple shot and letting the club do the work. There will be a little roll on the lofted-club short shots unless the green is soft almost to the stage of muddiness. It is only the hard-hit long shot with a lofted club, taking a divot in front of the ball, that has a lot of backspin on it when it hits the green.

The experts who have spent hours and hours and hours experimenting and practicing can play the short shots that spin back, but such nicely executed shots aren't in the repertoire of the average golfer and their absence is no great loss to him, as he isn't very often past the hole unless he tops an approach and sends it skidding far beyond the target.

PUTTING

Every golf veteran who reads or hears about a tournament pro coming out of a slump or emerging from mists of anonymity to win a tournament expects the happy winner to say something about the discovery of a new putting method. Then there is the laugh about the lucky guy going to keep the "secret" to himself. A few weeks pass and the "secret" is lost but not missed, since it didn't prove to be any great permanent treasure.

With all golfers and their putting, hope springs eternal and each man or maid has beautiful and swiftly fleeting visions of finding the can't-miss way of putting. I have had those dreams myself. I've optimistically used putters and manners of putting that I thought were the perfect answers. Putters that I used in winning the U. S., British, Canadian and Western Open and PGA Championships were given away two or three weeks after they'd served me as magic wands. They had lost their cunning. Me? I was as skilled as ever. It was the fickle putter playing me false. Generally I'd come back to a type of putter with a bit of a flange on the bottom of the blade and that seemed to serve me best longest.

I had the first of these putters changed a little. Eventually it became known as the Tommy Armour type of putter and for years has been a big seller. I might add that it has been used by several great golfers who are better putters than I ever was.

Why I never became the greatest putter in golf history I cannot understand. I studied the subject and really organized my research on it in a scholarly, scientific sort of way. I made quite a project of trying to substitute method for nerves. Having been in immensely more critical situations as a soldier than I'd ever find myself in as a golf championship contender, I was (or thought I was) in a condition to be immune to the tensions of make-believe combat, which is the essence of sport. I wasn't the only one who learned later that I'd get just as putter punch-drunk as anybody. Lloyd Mangrum, who knocked around considerably as a World War II combatant, and an admirable icily-nerved fellow, told a golf writer after winning the 1946 National Open—the first one after World War II—that he wasn't aware of any tension during the conventional 72 holes or the 36-hole play-off with Byron Nelson and Vic Ghezzi. "I knew I was lucky and in here on a pass, so what did I have to worry about?" Mangrum said. In later years he shivered on those short putts, even as you and I.

In my putting research I tried every grip and stance, cross-handed and between-the-feet methods, left-handed, looking-at-the-hole-instead-of-the-ball style, every sort of wrist or shoulder style, and every type of putter known in the free world. After years and thousands of investigations and tests in practice and competition, I always returned to the fundamentals as the only reliable factors of good putting.

The fundamentals are, simply, keeping the head dead steady and keeping the face of the putter absolutely across the line of the putt. Keeping the head dead steady is the hardest thing to do but you haven't much of a

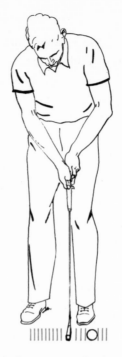

Keep the face of the putter absolutely square along the line of the putt all the way and through the ball

chance to stroke the putt precisely unless your head is still. All the rest is the trimming, good and useful a lot of times but not essential in every individual case.

Get yourself a nice putter that you like and that feels so well balanced it's almost like making your arms longer and rolling the ball with your hands. You'll find that the putter that suits you is one that has its sole flat on the ground while you are standing comfortably and with your hands rather close to your body. Something else that you'll learn is the "sweet spot" on the putter face where the putter should contact the ball.

What position the ball is in with relation to your feet

may be a matter of individual preference. I've seen some very good putters play the ball about in line off the left toe, and some about in the middle of the stance; a few off the right toe. One thing that almost all of them do is to have their eyes about over the ball.

A lot of the good putters say that they swing the putter back with the left hand and in that way keep the putter face from getting dangerously outside the direction line, and stroke the putt with the right hand, with the right arm sliding across the ribs.

The majority of the good putters of this period tap the putts of ten feet or shorter and stroke the longer putts. Nearly all of them have the back of the left hand going squarely toward the hole and are careful not to have the wrists bend so the right hand gets ahead of the left as the putt is stroked. All of the tournament players take pains to keep the right wrist from rolling over the left, because this takes the putter face badly off the required right angle to the direction line. For this protection they grip the putter with the palms almost facing outward.

The grip, with very few exceptions, is a finger grip. It has to be to get the delicate touch that instinctively adjusts the strength to the distance. Whether the grip is a four-fingers-and-thumbs hold, or a Vardon grip or a reverse Vardon with all the fingers of the right hand on the shaft, or with the right forefinger down the back of the shaft as a rudder, with the left thumbnail dug into the grip, or with any other arrangement your genius, comfort and hopes may devise, depends entirely on you. Despite the years I've spent trying to get the ideal putting method, you may come up with something I never thought of in my thousands of experiments. If it works for you keep at it until it goes sour.

Putting practice is a deceptive art. I doubt that there are a half dozen golfers out of about eight million in the United States who know how to practice putting. And I'm not one of them now, although I used to think that I was concentrating on one element of procedure so it would become habitual, or automatic, and wouldn't have to be considered when I was playing for keeps. Most putting practice is merely spending time on getting the feel of holding the club with the fingers, and when that sensation is acquired it is very valuable on all clubs. Golf is a game of delicacy and clubhead speed, and not of brute force; so when you have the nerves of your fingertips telling the clubface what to do you have a big part of the shot-making problem solved.

I've told elsewhere about the greatest putting practice lesson I ever got and that was from Walter Travis, the Australian transplanted to the United States. In 1904 he became the first "outsider" to win the British Amateur. He didn't have much of a long game, so he did it by rolling putts right through the hearts of the opponents. Travis told me that he placed four balls starting at a distance of 3 feet east, west, north and south of the hole, and putted them. If he holed all four, he went back 6 inches. When he had finally missed one of these balls—perhaps when the four balls were each 8 feet from the cup—he would start the routine all over from 3 feet. That impressed on me the importance of being careful, and carefulness in each detail of organization is a great deal of fine putting.

Nothing is more frustrating or agonizing than putting

because it places such a tremendous premium on such a short distance. You can hit a drive 300 yards, and on the scorecard, missing a putt of 10 inches more than loses whatever edge your fine drive gave you. That's a shame but that's the game, and you are not going to change it, so you'd better go along and play the percentage that favors the good putter.

You've got to protect yourself against the common fault of stopping the clubhead before you've got your putterface through the ball at a right angle to the direction line. One good way of protecting yourself against failure to finish the putt is to do what Bill Casper does. Casper is one of the finest putters golf has seen and a great golfer in other departments, too. He always goes through the putt with the back of his left hand leading toward the hole. Most of the excellent putters are what you might call left-handed putters. There is less chance of stopping and distorting putterface direction when you have a firm left wrist.

Quitting

Quitting on a shot happens much more frequently than you might ever believe. I've been watching the average sort of golfer carefully for many years and my estimate is that it takes place in about 60 out of every 100 shots he takes. He quits because he is afraid. If you want to go into the simple logic of this failure to complete the shot, the quitting golfer is afraid because he is ignorant. He simply doesn't know what to do when he gets the clubhead to the ball. He probably has only a dim idea of how he happened to get close to doing the job.

The fault of quitting afflicts experts, too. I remember one critical exhibition vividly. It was long ago, too, but the case blew away a chance for a championship. It was at the 1935 National Open at Oakmont. That was the one Sam Parks won with 299. Jimmy Thomson was second with 301. Jimmy got to the 14th in the fourth round and was running smoothly. He hit an enormous drive, just about hole-high and to the left of the green. All he had left was a simple little pitch, one of those you've got to hit delicately but firmly with your hands or you're wrecked. But our Jimmy quit on the shot and fluffed it into a bunker, and there was a disastrous five.

He looked up a trifle too soon. Looking up as a form of quitting on the shot. Stay down to the shot until you've finished your work. When you lift your head you try to execute the shot with a body heave instead of standing still and hitting with your hands as you should.

Parenthetically, I can say again to some of the patriarchs in golf that the Parks victory in that 1935 National Open was not the amazing thing that a lot of fellows thought it was, but was one of the impressive psychological lessons in golf. Parks had played Oakmont so much that, although he was professional at the South Hills club in suburban Pittsburgh, you could almost say that Oakmont was pretty nearly his home course. Rarely does a professional win on his home course. Perhaps he gets careless or the championship strain seems to change the course for him. But whether there is or isn't something to the home course curse, it didn't mean a thing to the unscared Parks who played his four rounds in two strokes under the 301 at which Harry Cooper and I had tied in 1927. I won the play-off with a 76 to Harry's 79 in those pre-wedge, furrowed trap, deep rough, hard green days, so that gives you a reasonably clear idea that Parks won on a testing course.

The moans about courses being "monsters" for modern National Open championships entertain me. A few of us, in what were the romantic if not the fiscal "Golden Days" of tournament golf, sobbed about the horrors of a course that was designated to determine which one of us happened to be the best player for the conventional four rounds of the National Open. However, the seasoned majority regarded the course as one of the major elements in the test, involving skill, brains, luck and heart and we saw no reason to be afraid of what an architect could do to us if he risked distorting the values of the game. Westbrook Pegler, the sports writer, cured an old friend of mine of the habit of jumping into print with the charge that the course on which the National Open championship was to be played was unfair, conceived in iniquity and bred in sin. Mr. Pegler suggested that the critic, if he didn't like the course on which fame and fortune was offered, should join the club, if acceptable as a member, then pay dues and assessments and have the course changed to meet the critic's likes. Come to think of it, possibly complaining about the course is a manner of quitting.

With even the greatest golfers quitting on shots, you might think that a cure for quitting would be discovered by this time, but there has been no progress in that direction. The best you can expect is to not make a habit of quitting, although you may have that fault choke you now and then.

Quitting is the result of tension and that is developed by the body. When you tighten in your body you become unable to throw your hands through the shot and it becomes a body hit and hasn't got much authority at the moment of contact.

Holding the club tightly also contributes to quitting. A grip that has the tips of the last three fingers of the left hand controlling the club and the middle two fingers of the right hand curled around the club gently but in correct position, will strengthen instinctively and whip the club into and after the ball. The tight grip has a tendency to freeze or collapse the instant the clubhead strikes the ball.

Rhythm

R hythm in golf is the smooth flow of developing details of the swing. It coordinates every element so there is no jerkiness or neglect of any part of the performance but orderly progress to the completion of the job. Rhythm and timing in golf are almost synonymous. The rhythm varies in pace being, generally, comparatively slow in the backswing, coming almost to pause at the top of the backswing, then accelerating in the downswing until the hit is the emphatically accented stage of movement. The follow-through is an echo of the effective rhythm.

It is rhythm that makes a golf swing beautiful and an expression of a true artist. There are some excellent golfers whose swings are smooth, and every detail is perfectly synchronized, yet their swings have a mechanical look. Those swings are hard work and only for the few who can devote a tremendous amount of time to perfecting them and keeping them together.

The most rhythmic swing I ever saw was that of Bob Jones. It seemed to flow like pouring honey. I never saw him hurrying a swing or off balance when he hit a shot. Poetry of motion was in every shot Jones played. His timing was so perfect that he always allowed himself enough time to complete every one of the necessary moves of feet, legs, body, shoulders, arms and hands, and when you think of what tiny fractions of instants are allotted for that coordination you realize what a wonderful thing the Jones swing was.

Rhythm comes from perfect muscular control. Muscular control may be instinctive or deliberate or both during a golf swing, and it is the reason why you are able to hit the ball. Our muscles instinctively are trying to whack the clubhead against the ball, but often we seem to have a devilish determination to interfere with the impulse. Consequently we are inclined to fight ourselves and rush to hit at the ball before we are ready. Waiting until we get ready is the essential to good timing in golf and we get that all-important pause at the top of the backswing. It is that pause that allows the golfer to finish the backswing. The ordinary golfer seldom completes his backswing before he starts down with a jerk, throwing himself out of balance and aim.

There are discussions about this pause because it is often imperceptible, and once in a while a good player will say that he is not aware of this tiny stop for change of direction of the club. Yet that same man, viewing slow motion pictures of his swing, sees his hands and the club-head clearly held still one small fraction of a second before the downswing is started.

The pause at the top is the key to effective timing. It is essential syncopation of the rhythm of a good swing. You've got to have it. It is insurance against throwing away power at the top of your swing where you can't use power. This pause is one of the differences between the swings of the experts and the efforts of inept golfers. It helps to control the pace of the swing so that the club-head is moving swiftest as the ball is being hit.

Stance

tand correctly in relation to the ball or you make golf unnecessarily difficult and risky. That should be obvious to anyone who thinks at all about how good golf has to be played. It is amazing how careless most golfers are about the way they place their feet in relation to the ball, and how this carelessness is the cause of bad aiming and failure to use clubs effectively. The fellow who would very carefully aim a gun at a target one hundred feet away won't even place his clubface behind the ball, make sure it is squarely across the direction line, then arrange his feet, body and hands in proper relation to the ball, so the swing will be quite accurately in the required path.

Clubs are designed to be used with a correct stance. You cannot get results from a club unless your stance adjusts it rather precisely to its work. The skilled club-maker designs and manufactures clubs to be used with a swing that is fundamentally the same for every shot, except for the power required for each shot. Hence the type of the shot is determined to a great extent by where the arc of the swing brings the "sweet spot" of the club-face into precise contact with the ball.

The basic position for the ball with a normal lie is half-way between the inner edges of the heels, the heels about as far apart as the shoulder tips, the hands to be approximately in the same plane as the ball. With the club soled flat on the ground and the middle of the face of the club squarely back of the ball, angle and length of the club determine the distance of the feet from the imaginary direction line that runs through the ball. The arms should hang down comfortably so the hands are

THE SQUARE STANCE
For fairway woods

fairly close to the body. Posture is fairly erect, with the knees loose and bent a trifle. The main departure from vertical is at the neck. There's no stooping, stretching or squatting in the posture that permits a free body turn and retains stability. The left arm and the shaft are practically in line, with no break at the wrists.

This basic stance is square, that is, with toes on a line parallel with the direction line, and turned out slightly as one normally stands. This square stance with the ball in the middle position is the stance for the fairways woods and the 5-iron and irons of lesser loft. The stance favored for the teed-up drive has the ball between a line slightly to the right of the left heel and the middle of the stance. The hands are a bit behind the plane of the clubface. The closed stance usually is used for the drive. With your right foot slightly farther from the direction

THE SQUARE STANCE
For long irons

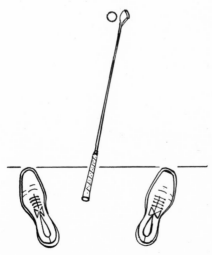

line than the left foot is, you allow yourself more freedom for turning your body, and set yourself so you can bring the club down inside the direction line and whip the clubhead toward the target.

Often the average golfer has the ball teed in a line off the left toe, or even a bit farther to the left. Then it is physically impossible to drive without falling into the ball. When you lunge into the ball almost anything but a good shot can happen, and the most frequent misfiring is a skied drive. Then the player tells himself that he teed the ball too high and hit under it. He has a mark of ball paint on the top of his driver as what he thinks is proof of the accuracy of his diagnosis. But what actually happened was that the club turned as he fell into the ball and he hit with the forward part of the top of the club.

The right foot should be turned slightly to the right

THE CLOSED STANCE
For the teed-up drive

when you're playing from a closed stance. That little bit of pointing outward by your right foot will ease the strain on your right thigh, and probably on your entire back, because you have to twist around plenty as well as use exceedingly energetic perfectly-timed hand action to generate power for your drive. Unless your feet are in position to minimize strain on your back muscles and your spine, you are inviting injury. Young players who are strong and flexible can get away with severe strain on the back for a while but eventually it catches up with them. I certainly don't qualify as an expert on anatomy, but as a studious observer of footwork (or the lack of it) in golf I long ago noticed that the fellows whose foot placement and foot action tightened them from the ground up were the golfers who complained the most about back trouble. The older golfer ought to be especially careful to arrange his feet in relation to the ball so he can move his body freely and without undue strain in winding up for his shot. That's quite a job and not simply one of the minor details of golf.

The right foot at a right angle to the direction line is correct for the shorter shots that are mainly arm and hand hits rather than swings culminating in hitting. I've observed that many ordinary golfers think they have the right foot at 90 degrees to the direction line, but actually are standing pigeon-toed and aggravating the strain on the back as they turn. Furthermore, this square or pigeon-toed position often accounts for "coming down over the ball," which means coming from outside the direction line and sliding the clubface in and across the ball, lessening the impact of the shot and producing a sweeping, sickening slice.

THE OPEN STANCE
For the short irons

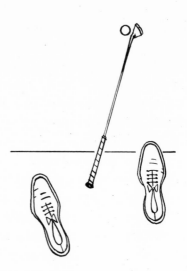

There never is any debate about toeing the left foot outward. Instinctively you set your left foot so you unlock yourself and give yourself a chance to turn into the shot. Frequently there is a tendency to have the left foot too far from the direction line and the stance opened too much for an accurate medium-length shot. Simply turning the left foot out with both feet toeing the direction line takes care of the situation on those shots. On the shorter pitch shots your left foot is drawn back so that your body is almost 45 degrees to the direction line. You don't need body action in those shots, merely freedom of the shoulders and absence of tension anywhere. And on all the shorter shots you have to remember that the weight is accented on the left foot at address and stays there all through the stroking.

You probably will get an impressive lesson on the importance of precision in location of the feet in relation to the ball when your driving is not satisfactory, and you've been trying all sorts of complicated cures. Simply make sure that the ball is in the middle of the stance and you'll probably start connecting solidly, even though that middle location is a trifle more to the right than you need to get the ideal results.

On the fairway shots with the woods and the irons up to the 7-iron the middle position of the ball is the correct one. With the ball and the feet in that relative position your stance helps you to connect with the ball when you are on the downswing.

You'll have to experiment in learning what's the correct distance between your feet for the various shots. As a general rule the longer the shot, the wider apart the feet should be, within reasonable limits. When the feet are too far apart you probably will lock your body on the backswing and sway instead of turn. On the long irons (the 2-, 3- and 4-iron) your feet should be closer than they are for the woods. And, by the way, for the average golfer the 5-wood is an easier club to play than the 2-iron is.

Your feet get closer together as the club loft increases when you are making fairway or rough shots. In the sand and using a sand wedge your feet are about the same distance apart as they'd normally be when you stand at ease. The safest arrangement with a normal lie in sand that is not wet or fluffy is to have the ball on the middle line between your feet. When you have to get the ball rising quickly to clear a near and steep bank you can move back a trifle so the ball is a bit to the left of center of the stance.

In standing for inclined lies, figure the line the clubface will have to follow connecting with the ball. Then you see how you will have to balance yourself so you can hit from a steady position.

You'll probably slice a downhill shot so aim the shot to the left, open your stance, play the ball a trifle to the left of center and use a club stronger than you'd use for the same distance from a normal lie. With the lie uphill, close your stance, allow for a hook, have the ball slightly to the right of center and use the same club you would use with a level lie.

When the ball is lying lower than your feet on a sidehill slope, play it about as you would a shot from a downhill lie and "sit down" a trifle to it so you have the feeling you are solid on your feet—maybe a bit heavier on your heels—and won't fall forward. Take a club one number less than you'd use for a normal lie. With the ball higher than your feet on a sidehill slope, hold your club lower on the grip. That will shorten your swing so use a club stronger than you'd normally use.

Good balance is absolutely essential on incline lies and when you arrange for that you will maintain your stability by hitting with your hands instead of making the average player's error of trying to hit these shots with the body. With firm balance assured by sensible footwork, you can hit these sidehill shots more easily and they will go better.

Traps

The one shot in golf that you can buy is a good shot out of a bunker onto a green. When the sand wedge with its inclined flange came into the game there no longer remained a fine art in getting out of a trap. The shot became as nearly a fool-proof job of mechanics as you can get in golf.

You generally have an allowance for a generous margin of error in the sand wedge shot in a bunker. Often a variation of as much as an inch in the distance you hit behind the ball won't mean a ruinous difference. The main thing the average golfer has to think about in using the sand wedge is getting out of the trap. He shouldn't allow himself to worry about how close to the hole he is going to get, or any of the details of the execution of the shot. To apply an observation from politics—in making a wedge shot out of the sand all the golfer has to fear is fear itself. The expert frequently has more confidence in his sand wedge than he does in his putter. He knows there isn't much to making the wedge shot. In the hands of the expert the wedge is a deadly weapon, and a versatile one, too.

I had the interesting and pleasant experience of seeing a promising, intelligent young golfer base his tactical policy on his command of the wedge and become a two-time National Open winner and one of our finest golfers. When I first saw Julius Boros play he had a graceful swing but a somewhat timid manner of going at the target. There was one thing he did have early, and has maintained since. That is the best command of the wedges—the sand wedge and the pitching wedge—that I've ever seen, even though every top bracket professional and hundreds of the better amateurs are amazingly consistent in their excellence on these shots. I counseled Julius to change his thinking and his style of play and go boldly for the hole on the long approaches. Although he might misfire on some of his shots to the pin, he was so adept with the wedges that he'd have a very good chance of getting down in two from almost anywhere he landed around the green. This proved to be the case. The Boros display of the versatility of the wedge was especially brilliant at the Country Club of Brookline, when he made wedge shots from the deep, tangled rough so close to the hole he saved himself several strokes and won the 1963 National Open.

The sand wedge, with its wide sole and its 55 degree loft, its heavy head and its short shaft, is one of the handiest as well as easiest of tools for the ordinary golfer who is in trouble. Not only the sand shots but shots from the rough, and difficult close lies, are recovery shots you have bought cheaply when you have a wedge in your bag. Yet, despite the simplicity of learning to use the wedge well, I rarely have known for an ordinary golfer who took a half-hour lesson on a wedge, then practiced wedge shots in various sorts of sand, variegated lies in sand or rough, or in other situations for which the club is made to perform.

I have seen professionals who have had plenty of trouble and frustration trying to teach shot-making with other clubs to pupils, but I've never known an instructor who needed more than one half hour to teach a fairly intelligent and physically normal man, woman or youngster how to use the sand wedge well. Firmness rather than power, a steady head, a shoulder turn instead of a turn from the hips, cocking of the wrists early in the backswing, a straight left arm that swings through the whole shot to a full follow through—these are the points that

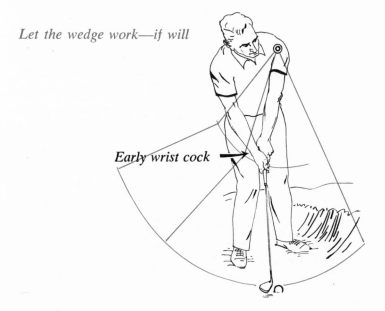

Let the wedge work—if will

Early wrist cock

make a first class trap shot. There's nothing complex about these elements.

But let's take the case of the Unhappy Example trying to get out of a bunker somewhere near the hole. The first mistake he makes is to be in a hurry. He pays no attention to where his feet are in relation to the ball and what the consistency of the sand is—hard, coarse, sugary, wet or dry. He neglects to get his feet settled in the sand so he can stand with stability and turn his shoulders without shaking his head. Usually he is holding the club in a vise-like clutch. When he begins to swing he subconsciously loosens his connection and he lets up on the shot, chops down into the sand, and quits or opens the face of the club. As a result the ball skids off to the right in an almost shanked shot. He goes to a lot of trouble to do everything wrong when he is playing a club that works perfectly with the most ordinary of fairly good swings.

If your tendency is to make a rather quick-rising shot close to the bank of the bunker, play the ball about in line with your left heel with a slightly open stance and your feet a little closer together than they'd be for a medium-length iron shot. Aim a bit to the left of the hole, because the ball with the outside-in line of the swing through the sand is going to spin a bit to the right.

Always remember that this trap shot, like all other precision shots, is left hand controlled, so keep the back of your left hand going toward the target. Keep your right elbow down and close to your ribs. The flying right elbow, a result of the panic experienced by the fellow who erroneously thinks the trap shot is tough, accounts for many of the badly-played bunker shots, just as it is the cause of many other poor approaches.

Distribution of the weight is important in getting the swing in the correct arc. Understand that you have to get the sand wedge swinging under the ball; thus the sand almost becomes a part of the clubface.

For the rather quick-rising shot out of the sand, the weight at address should be about equal on both feet and not change as you are making the shot. You keep your head steady and swing the club with your arms and hands. That doesn't require any shifting of weight as is required by a pronounced turn of the body.

When you have a sand-trap shot from an ordinary, slightly buried lie, and of moderate trajectory, play the ball from about the middle of your slightly open stance. That means that your right foot will be slightly closer than your left to the direction line, and you will be facing the hole somewhat. That will restrict your swing a little bit, but it will help your follow-through. For this shot keep your weight accented on your left foot.

The follow-through of a sand trap shot is very im-

portant. You don't dare quit on that shot. You've got to get the club cutting down through the sand, with the sand forcing the ball up and on its way, or you have one of those unnecessarily wasted shots for which you pay not only blood, sweat and bad language, but one or two strokes you easily and intelligently might have saved. As there is no footwork and no pivot, and just enough body action in the sand trap shot to keep you from stiffening, you realize the stroke is primarily a hand shot. That means you break your wrists early in the backswing, pull your hands close together down to the hitting sector, then throw your hands through the shot. There are no soft shots out of the sand. In that respect they are like the short putts with a tiny bit of incline. You must tap them firmly along the direct line to the hole to make them; but if you delicately try to "baby" them along a curved route only the merciful Allah makes the putt for you.

The one way to learn how much power to put into the sand trap shot, and where to hit the leading edge of the wedge into the sand, is by practice. Only you can determine how to play the shot from various sorts of lies and various kinds of sand. I can tell you that when your ball is in what's called a "fried egg lie," and sunk in the center of an encircling depression, the general rule is to hit into the rim of the depression farthest from the hole and keep swinging through, but my million words won't have the same educational value that your few successful applications will.

When the ball is lying on an up-slope in the sand, play it about in a line off your left instep and open the clubface a little so that you will splash the ball up with the sand. When the ball is lying downhill in the sand, turn the face of the club over a trifle so it is slightly hooded, play the ball a bit to the right of the center of your stance, and hit into the sand a little further back of the ball than you'd do for a level lie. Then you will have the clubface starting to come up in its path under the ball.

Although the sand wedge is the most reliable tool to use under normal conditions out of traps guarding greens, there are cases of good lies, smoothly packed sand, and bunkers that slope from the level of the green to the sand, where you can putt across the sand, up the short grass of the bank of the bunker and finish reasonably close to the hole. If that is the simplest way, and involves the least mental or physical risk, you certainly ought to use your putter and not a wedge for the shot. There is no rule in the book that prohibits use of the putter for a trap shot or for an approach when the grass between your ball and the green is short and even. Those rolling shots from as far as 15 yards off the green make good sense when the surface is favorable to their fairly accurate travel. The chief things to bear in mind in executing these putter shots are to maintain an absolutely steady head and both hands working together in a low backswing, and a follow through that keeps the face of the putter squarely across the line to the hole. The tendency of the ordinary golfer is to jerk these putter approaches with a right hand flip that rolls the right hand over the left and tops the ball. You have to practice a lot of these shots until you develop the "touch" for the distance required.

Sometimes a chip shot with a 6- or 7-iron out of a good lie in the sand is the shot to play. In chipping or putting out of a trap you must hit the ball before your club gets into the sand. You have to play these shots with more accuracy than the wedge requires, so don't try these somewhat exacting shots unless you've practiced them enough to have a clear idea of what you have to do to get the result you want.

The longer shots from traps flanking fairways are made just as those shots would be made from turf. If the ball is slightly buried in the sand, play it a trifle to the right of center of your stance so you will be sure to be hitting down at the ball, getting the leading edge of the club under it. Then keep going through the shot so sand will be taken in the manner of a divot. Usually the average golfer tries to get too much distance with his fairway bunker shots and uses a club that hasn't got enough loft to clear the far bank of the trap safely. Time after time I have seen an ordinary player take a wood club in a bunker and with a mighty heave knock the ball into the rim of the bunker, and then curse it, as it dribbles back into the sand. He has not only lost a stroke, but he is worse off for the next shot than before because he is closer to the edge of the trap. Even if his 3-, 4-, or 5-wood shot had sailed up over the mound of the bunker he wouldn't have been on the green. He would have needed another shot. Why didn't he use his brains and play out surely and easily, say with a 5-iron, then take another easy iron shot to the green, instead of trying to make enough distance with a risky wood shot to use a 7- or 8-iron?

One of the first lessons a man or woman should learn about golfing tactics is that when it is going to take two shots to make the green, make both shots easy ones. Especially when the pitching wedge is available and quite reliable for the typical golfer, the approach shots of 75 yards or shorter should be nothing to worry about.

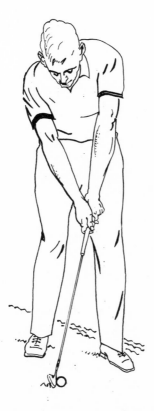

Hit with your hands *and stay steady*

The wedge is a wonder-working club out of deep rough. You play the ball a little to the right of the middle of your stance because you must have a rather upright swing. Come down in a sharp arc that eases your job of chopping through the grass and under the ball. You've got to have a firm grip with your fingers in making the shot out of the long rough because the grass is going to twist around your clubhead and smother the shot unless you keep the edge of the wedge clearing the way.

There isn't much skill required for playing a fairly good pitch shot with wedge. Your feet are only a few inches apart. Your stance is open. Your weight is mainly on your left foot and it stays there. The ball is played about in line with your left heel. Your hands are slightly in front of the ball at address and they're comfortably close to your body. Keep your head steady and swing your hands and arms through the shot.

Unity

Unity is a tremendously important word in the lexicon of golf, but you seldom hear or see it, although you must have unity in your swing or you haven't an effective, dependable swing. Unity is the quality of oneness that brings all details together in harmony. One of the definitions of "unity" in my Webster's is, "a combination or ordering of parts in a literary or artistic production that . . . promotes an undivided total effect." Other definitions are, "a condition of harmony" and, "a totality of related parts." The golfer who has just hit a grand shot and says "I had everything working for me" has said that he hit a unified shot, in which everything was working in coordination.

To get unity into your game, start by thinking of your two hands. Golf is a two-handed game. You have to have both of them working together or you'll never be much of a golfer. Among the broad generalities in golf are those of the left hand (and arm and side) being for direction and the right-side elements for power. This is true, but unless they're both working closely together the left won't be reliable in steering the shot, and the right won't supply satisfactory distance, regardless of what the required length may be.

You have to think of the elements of a golf stroke as something like matrimony: they are both "togetherness" arrangements with everything coordinated and operating in harmony. But you will not often see those ideal arrangements among mere mortals. There is seldom a golfer who is so perfect that he gets everything geared together exactly right. In the years I've played, taught and observed golf I've seen possibly ten extraordinarily fine golfers, and I surmise that each of them would admit that he had played not more than three nearly per-

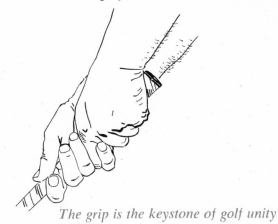

The grip is the keystone of golf unity

fect rounds in his life. There always seems to be a flaw in the picture. Just one part is not as it should be, and doesn't fit. The footwork, hand action, timing or balance may be the slightest trifle out of order, and that costs strokes.

The average player doesn't realize that when he has his good days the departments are working in unison. The expert knows from painful experience that on the day when he "doesn't have it" at least one of the components is missing. When you are not playing well you have to examine yourself to determine which of the parts isn't functioning to make up the necessary unity, and, frankly, you probably will be lucky if you learn what the trouble is. Even the best of them are often unable to locate the fault, although the flaw may be obvious to a trained observer.

There is really little you can do about getting everything integrated smoothly again. The only practical suggestion I can make is an answer I've given hundreds of times when golfers have asked me, "What am I doing wrong?" I reply to the bewildered ones, "I don't know all you may be doing wrong, but I can tell you very positively what you are not doing right." Then we get to the positive treatment, and by stressing one essential, usually some of the other parts fall into place.

The indefinable essential of "touch" is the origin of unity. Some days the experts feel the club so well it seems to be virtually an extension of their fingers, and gives them such delicacy that putting is a pleasure. Other times you feel as though you were holding the club with boxing gloves and trying to swing with three arms. The expert, by long practice and play and possibly by aptitude, educates himself in the sensations required by a thoroughly coordinated stroke. The average player has to depend on a benevolent natural order of things, and merely tries to keep himself as free as he can from the heavy pressure that diminishes that nice touch so important to good golf.

I have a great deal of understanding and sympathy for the average golfer who had difficulty in adjusting his fingers, palms and wrists so that he gets and retains the desirable feel of the club. He (or she) may think he has trouble in this department, but I've been even more perplexed in some instruction problems. To sense the degree and location of feeling in, say, the partially concealed left hand and fingers of a pupil requires empathy more or less natural to the understanding teacher, and developed by his years of experience with students of various physical and temperamental characteristics.

The touch, or feeling, that unites the components of a golf shot into first class results, is primarily instinctive. On that account some are naturally quite good golfers, and others have to acquire and apply the sensations empirically. There is no more reason for hoping that you or anyone else can become a great golfer without a basis of instinctive ability than that you could become a famous passer in professional football merely by day-dreaming like Walter Mitty.

It often interests me to see what complex things are wonderfully well done when deliberate thinking is out of the act. For instance, there is the performance of dealing a deck of cards four different distances and directions, with each card being of minutely small thickness, the fingers of the left hand pushing out the cards in correct order and the fingers and forearm of the right hand distributing the cards with what is actually astonishing accuracy, if you stop to think about it, which, providentially, you don't.

I have found myself in the paradoxical situation of teaching intelligent men, men who have superior capacity for thought, and wishing that they wouldn't think so much. I wanted them to relax and allow their instincts to tie everything together. In these instances I have thought of what a veteran pro friend of mine said about the hardest part of his teaching work being to get his pupils to stop worrying and give a good swing a chance to happen.

A good golf swing happens too fast for more than two details to be fitted together deliberately while the swing is under way. The ordinary golfer is lucky if he can apply just one idea while he is in action. So he has to be particularly careful about the fundamental positions of grip and address, for he is able to attend to these before he ever starts to swing. For when the swing begins, who knows what is going to happen and why? The mysteries of scoring are sometimes beyond understanding. As examples of these puzzles I recall the first two rounds played by Craig Wood in the 1936 Masters. Craig started with an 88. His next round was 67. The moral of those historic rounds seems to be, "Don't surrender when your game falls apart; maybe tomorrow you can put the pieces together and be 21 strokes better." There is no rule against hoping.

Vagaries

Vagaries in golf—those unpredictable manifestations of the character of the game and its players—should teach you to expect the unexpected and be calm when it happens. You never know when a break is going for you or against you. I suppose luck has been a lady to me more times than she's been an enemy, yet I'm like every other golfer in remembering the bad bounces and in suspecting that the favorable accidents are for the other fellow.

The greatest players hit bad shots at the worst times. Arnold Palmer got a 12 on the 9th hole at the Rancho municipal course during the 1961 Los Angeles Open. He sliced two fairway woods out of bounds, then hooked two out. Ben Hogan, certainly one of the greatest golfers of all time, had a delicate little pitch across a stream to the 17th hole in the last round of the 1960 National Open at Cherry Hills. It was a shot that Hogan could play better than any other golfer who ever lived. He was going for a birdie 4. But the unbelievable happened. The imperturbable one, who was called by admiring Scots "The Wee Ice Mon," knocked that brave shot into the far bank and it dribbled down to the edge of the creek. He got a 6. He finished four strokes behind Palmer, the winner of that championship, who started his last round with a drive that a very fortunate bounce kept from rolling into a little brook.

Francis Ouimet was a youth who was well aware of the vagaries of golf. In telling about winning the 1913 National Open when he defeated the British masters, Harry Vardon and Ted Ray, in the play-off and gave golf in the United States an immense boost, Ouimet related hitting a shot to the blind 8 green. He said he wanted to believe his caddie who told him the ball was stone dead but said to the lad that it wasn't inches away, but that he thought he'd have a chance to hole his 3. "You see I did not wish to be disappointed," recalled Ouimet, and that pessimistic attitude isn't bad policy. It kept him from being upset when things really did go against him. In the third round he slopped out through the rain for a 43 and had nearly abandoned hope. Now let me quote Oiumet in citing vagaries of golf:

The tenth hole was a par three. Owing to the sodden condition of the putting green a high pitch was dangerous because the ball would become imbedded in the soft turf. I elected to use a jigger, intending to hit a low shot to the green. I forgot to look at the ball and hit it about 15 feet. I put my next on the green about eight feet from the hole and then took three putts for an inglorious five . . . I heard one man say "It's too bad, he has blown up." I knew he meant me, and it made me angry. It put me in the proper frame of mind to carry on.

The other fellows were having trouble, too. Ouimet came back in 36 for a 79 that tied him with the British veteran stars at 304. In the play-off, young Ouimet scored 72 against Vardon's 77 and Ray's 78.

Golf's accidents can happen to the duffer's benefit, too. Of the 15,000 or more holes-in-one a year, the majority are made by average golfers. The most curious case I've heard about was that of a beginner who took his first drive on a small town nine-hole course in the northwest, and sliced from the first tee into the cup on the ninth green, completing the entire round in one shot. I intended to follow that man's career and see how he managed to improve.

There are 1001 fascinating uncertainties of golf. They all add up to "these things happen, so forget it and keep trying" if the accident was against you. Equally important, remind yourself that if you got the breaks you shouldn't become cocky until your score is officially recorded, and you are in the locker room letting down.

In the 1927 National Open at Oakmont I was leading by 5 shots and lost 6 strokes in 2 holes. At the 12th I hit two beautiful shots and the second went into one of those ribbed bunkers, and in the pre-wedge days it took me 3 to get out. And before I could put the pieces

together on the 14th hole and get back to normal, I'd
lost my lead.

At Oakmont the devil always was apt to jump up.
Phil Rodgers never will forget the 17th hole at Oakmont
in the 1962 National Open when he hit a ball into a
low tree to the left and short of the green, and whacked
at the ball until he'd lost his chance to win that championship. It didn't make any difference that golf archi-
tects and players said that the small evergreen at its location gave a Disneyland aspect to the famed golf course.
The tree was there, and it accounted for the two strokes
difference between Rodgers and the 283 at which the
eventual winner Nicklaus, and Palmer, the other man
in the play-off, tied.

I remember another vagary of golf that had Oakmont
as its scene, and me as the fellow on the lucky end. It
was during the 1927 National Open and even if I did
win, and should be coy, I think that was the toughest
course of all time. I made a bet with Johnny Rogers, a
very long hitting professional from Denver. Our wager
was twenty-five dollars a stroke. Johnny led the field
the first 9, going out in 34. I began to fear I'd be in the
hands of a creditor's committee. Then Johnny got a 6
on the 10th hole, 8 on the 11th, followed it with a 10
and got back in 56. That 90 was followed by an 83
and Johnny didn't qualify for the last 36 of the usual
route of the championship. I had 78, then 71 as my first
two rounds. There was no way on earth of explaining
24 strokes between Johnny and myself. If that much
difference had been imagined, there would have been no
bet. But that's the erratic nature of golf scoring.

The tales of the opposite of my experience with Rogers

are so numerous they remind you to keep swinging and not put the ball into your pocket. In a Metropolitan (New York) championship, shortly after I came to the United States, Alex Smith struggled to get 40 on the outgoing 9 and came back in 30. John Anderson, an outstanding amateur of that time, was out in 45, then pulled himself together for a 30 on the homeward-bound 9 during a Met Open.

There are days when you can't putt well but play every other shot wonderfully; and equally as mysterious are the times when you can hardly get off the tee and are all over the course, but you are putting so amazingly that you are still in the battle. I recall getting 64 in the last round of a Canadian Open championship to tie Leo Diegel (then win from him in the play-off). In the last round I missed six short putts—those 3- to 5-footers you must have to win. I holed only one long putt. But it seemed that on the rest of the holes every time I hit an iron the ball stopped right beside the hole. I've never been able to get the vaguest idea of why I've missed a 2-foot putt and then, at the next hole, rolled in a 40-footer. Maybe it's fate, not skill.

The experience of missing easy putts and holing the hard ones was mine at Carnoustie in winning a British Open. Those were my days; but on the last day the stars were wrong for José Jurado, the Argentinian, for he got to the 17th on the fourth round with a chance to pass me and win. But he hit behind a ball, knocked it about 120 yards into the water, and the show was over for him. José was an excellent iron player and a fine putter. Why he missed that one of all his iron shots is an enigma, for he was an experienced golfer of sound judgment and self-control in every respect. But he was hit with what happens in golf. On account of just one shot Jurado misplayed, I can remember without vain regrets missing a 2-foot putt on that hole after hitting a 2-iron up to the green. On the 16th hole I'd batted in a 40-footer, and I can't explain that, either.

If the vagaries of golf don't remind you to keep your head when things go wrong and to keep plugging along and waiting for a good break, you will miss one of the wonderful lessons of golf—and of living.

Waggle
and
Weight

When you realize that about 90 per cent of the better players have a waggle as the preliminary movement of the hands before hitting the ball, you must appreciate that this moving of the club back and forth is a swing in miniature that loosens them physically and mentally.

There is some kind of loosening preliminary that seems to be essential before the true golf swing is begun. Some have short, medium or long waggles and Doug Sanders, for instance, has no conventional waggle at all, but starts his swing from a stationary position of the clubhead back of the ball. However, I've noticed that just before his swing begins, his knees and body move a little to the left in a nearly imperceptible version of a forward press, and his hands are bound to go along with that action. Player also has a muscle-unlocking preliminary that is more of a forward press and rebound than it is a waggle, but it gets him started away smoothly and that's the idea of the waggle. The experts work out their own ways to waggle the club into a smooth-flowing backswing. Walter Hagen used to have a waggle that was big and easy, something like warming up for a trapeze act, then he quit that and adopted a stance that had his right knee turned decidedly toward the left in a kind of built-in forward press, and from that position he could shift weight gracefully in getting his backswing started. When I first saw Gary Player he had a peculiar wriggle of his feet which was a combination of waggle and forward press that was one of the most beautiful jobs I ever saw of getting a swing going in a velvety manner.

All that the waggle amounts to, mechanically, is moving the club back and forth with your hands—just a wee bit of shoulder and arm action and practically no independent movement of your wrists. But you have the feeling that your wrists have a nice muscle tone—neither tight nor flabby. Your grip is light. It is very, very light with your right hand. The left hand controls the waggle and reminds you right at the beginning that the left hand is the one for control, and the right hand is to put the power in later on when the club is coming into the ball.

When the waggle is properly effective it not only eases tension in the forearm and back muscles, but in all the muscles of the body. It is comparable to the wind-up of a baseball pitcher in smoothly arranging the action and reaction that generates and releases power. After

you waggle the club you must not stop dead as you
sole the club behind the ball, but maintain the rhythm.

In a way, the practice swing is an unrestrained waggle.
It flows beautifully through the imaginary ball. What a
completely delightful game golf would be if we could
hit the ball with the practice swing but when the ball
is down there to be hit something happens to the average
golfer. He gets tight and jerky. The waggle will somewhat minimize that tendency to siffen suddenly. The
expert hits the ball with his practice swing. The ordinary
golfer's practice swing and his actual swing are two different things. The waggle that banishes tension may be
the means of getting the smooth practice swing to flow
into the swing that hits the ball.

WEIGHT

Distribution of weight is a major factor in hitting a
good shot—or a bad one. It is impossible to become
a good golfer without correct weight distribution during the swing. You can do well with a short swing
of the Sanders type, or with a long one with the club
shaft at the top angling down a little from the hands,
but in both cases the distribution of weight is identical.

At the top of the swing of a drive, weight is slightly
heavier on the right foot. As your hips are turned and
your right leg is inclined slightly toward the target you
may have a feeling that you are bracing yourself on your
right leg and winding your swing around that leg as an
axis. In hitting the fairway woods, weight at address
and at the top of the swing is about evenly distributed.

When you are playing the irons your weight is accented on your left foot at address, and all the way through the shot.

It is easy to tell you, as I have, how to have your weight distributed; and I've told you how the experts do it, but I've noticed that the average player seldom pays much attention to shifting his weight. As you swing into the ball your weight is accented on your left foot. Your right knee is bending to the left and you've got a feeling

DISTRIBUTION OF WEIGHT ON THE DRIVE

At address   *At the top of the swing*

that the inner fore part of your right foot is almost pushing you so your left foot is digging into the ground. That sensation of transference of weight onto your left foot as you are coming into the ball calls for having your right knee unlocked. If that knee gets stuck you don't get the action you want in throwing the clubhead into the shot.

When you think of hip pivot rather than shoulder turn you will get your weight distributed easily and naturally. And when you turn your hips your shoulders are

DISTRIBUTION OF WEIGHT ON THE IRONS

At address   *Swinging into the hit*

bound to turn. But you can turn your shoulders without twisting your hips and that is why you may not be shifting your weight and getting your back into your swing. At the finish of all your shots—long, medium and short—your weight should be mainly on your left foot and your body turned facing the target. Complete the job of shifting your weight and you won't quit on your shot.

Transfer your weight onto the left foot as you start to come into the ball, and unlock the right knee

X-ray
Your
Game

X-ray your game. You must. Golf is an introspective game. You have to consider how you think and how you feel in learning how to improve. Nobody can do that for you. I have been baffled looking at the golf of eminently successful businessmen and wondering how they ever were able to make millions if their golf was an indication of their type of thinking.

Much golf is played in a disorganized, careless and thoughtless manner. Probably half the shots made by the average golfer are played merely because it is his turn to shoot. He doesn't use as much brains in most of his shots as he'd use to put the cat out for the night. I've looked at ordinary golfers take curious whacks in the general direction of the ball and I've been utterly unable

Choose the easiest *club for the shot you have planned*

to imagine what, if anything, is going through their minds. They can't possibly be having a clear notion of hitting the ball. I suspect they haven't any mental picture of where they are or what they want to do.

All golf, as Caesar said of Gaul, is divided into three parts. Golf's divisions are (1) the mental preparation for the shot, (2) the physical preparation, and (3) the execution of the shot. Frequently I have been of the opinion that the first of the three parts of the game is the source of more errors of omission than there are mistakes in performance.

Time after time I have seen players with weird grips, stances and swing make pretty good scores. These unconventional golfers do have a clear idea of what they want to do—hit the ball into the hole. Maybe their reactions are instinctive, or I can't know in what mysterious way the good Lord moves these wonders to perform, but I have seen fellows who have their minds set on hitting the ball make better shots than they know how to make.

Every shot you hit, hit with one specific idea perfectly clear in your mind even if the idea is simply the elementary "hit the ball." As simple as that idea is, it is a tremendous improvement over the mental void of the player who stands up and moves his arms and hopes in a blank sort of a way that the ball will be hit and go somewhere.

Yips

You've never run the full gamut of golfing experience until you've had "the yips." The yips is a brain spasm that impairs the short game. I have the faint distinction of having first applied that term to the distressing affliction, and I wish I'd never had the sorrowful experiences that gave me the yips, the jerks, the jumps and all those other variations of explosions and paralysis that were called perfectly terrible names until, restricted by convention and weakened by sorrow, I gave the disorder the label which came into common use. And certainly the yips themselves are in too common use. They make cousins of the mighty and the meek in golf.

Undoubtedly the most terrifying display of the yips occurs when a short putt should be made. Then, out of nowhere comes the malady that makes it impossible to function with controlled effort. The yips is a pernicious disease and one of the most difficult to eradicate of all golfing faults. There comes that ghastly time when, with the first movement of the putter, the golfer blacks out, loses sight of the ball, and hasn't the remotest idea of what to do with the putter or, occasionally, that he is holding a putter.

I had the interesting experience of seeing the yips grab the great Bob Jones and discussing the disease with him. We were in Pinehurst when Jones made the shocking admission, "I've got the yips!" Why I should have thought the immortal Bob was immune to the yips I can't remember. Everybody gets them.

One of the worst cases on record was that of Harry Vardon. A yips victim almost shivers when he reads in Vardon's book *How to Play Golf* the ordeal of the British genius who won six British Open and one U. S. Open championships.

I have never felt nervous when taking part in a golf tournament; this lack of confidence which overtook me when I was playing a short putt was something altogether worse than nervousness. As I stood addressing the ball, I would watch for my right hand to jump. At the end of about two seconds I would not be looking at the ball at all. My gaze would have become riveted on my right hand. I simply could not resist the desire to discover what it was going to do. Directly I felt that it was about to jump I would snatch at the ball in a desperate effort to play the shot before the involuntary movement could take effect. Up would go my head and body with a start and off would go the ball—anywhere but on a proper line. . . . I felt completely comfortable with putts of three yards or more and could play them satisfactorily. It was only when I got to within four feet of the hole that I became conscious of the difficulties. . . . I could always tell when I was about to have relief. If no jump visited me on the first green I knew I was safe for the round. As a generator of confidence I would recommend a course of putting in the dark. There is a lot of imagination in seeing a line all the way from the ball to the hole.

This Vardon book was first published in 1912. You can imagine how the greens were then compared to the smooth surfaces today so you can picture what a horrible thing an attack of the yips must have been then.

The Vardon description of the yips doesn't differ in substance from what Jones vividly described in telling me at Pinehurst what had happened to his putting.

"You've got the yips; no doubt in the world of it. And you'll never get rid of them," I commiserated with him.

The next spring at Augusta I asked Bob, "How are your yips?"

"I got rid of them," he said to my astonishment.

"How? What could you possibly do?"

"I don't look at the blade of the putter anymore. I just put the putter down, don't line up the blade and get it swinging," Jones explained.

And that was his version of the Vardon yips treatment of putting in the dark. But it wasn't completely successful. Yips don't seize the victim during a practice round. It is a tournament disease. During one of the early Masters I watched Jones in a seizure. On the first hole his approach was 20 feet from the hole. He lagged up to about 3 feet and eventually hit that short putt with agony and in spasm. On the 2nd hole he hit wonderful first and second shots and almost holed his approach. Then a frantic yip and a miss. And after playing magnificently to the green on the 3rd hole he yipped another putt. Bob had to continue to suffer. I couldn't stand to watch any longer.

Hogan got the yips and still has spells of them. From the tee to green Hogan for years has been one of the greatest golfers, perhaps the greatest. Although in his 50's, in tournament performances he is about as good as any of the younger bright stars, and often better, but he is often tragic on the short yipped putts. Before tournaments and in practice he will be holing the short ones, but when the competition is on, the man whom many (myself included) regard as having the finest nerve control in golf gets that mysterious uncertainty, the yips.

I have a hunch that the yips is the result of years of competitive strain, a sort of punch-nuttiness with the putter. The tension you experience during critical delicate putts finally seems to break you down. I got the yips so badly I quit tournament golf. The excitement and rewards weren't worth the pain the yips gave me.

There are some who get the yips on a one dollar to five dollar Nassau, although the money really doesn't mean a thing to them. As hosts they will cheerfully pick up one hundred dollars worth of club tabs for food, drink, caddies and green fees and tip liberally, but get a deadly attack of the yips when a two dollar 2-foot putt confronts them at the 18th green. Other typical golfers whose frugality is keener than their enjoyment of the game will jerk a putt in a pitiful seizure of the yips when a quarter is involved. Even seasoned hustlers are subject to the yips when the price is high enough.

We all know that all there is to holing short putts is to keep the head steady and have the clubface aimed so the ball will roll on the line to the hole. That's simple. Even after a yipped putt you can do the simple job again and correctly. Nothing at all has changed about the putt except the yips monster has turned you loose.

I had a 3-foot putt to win British Open championship. On the previous hole I'd made a ghastly effort and yipped a 2-footer that missed. Now on the 72nd green three feet away from victory I took a new grip, holding the club as tightly as I could and with stiff wrists, and took a different stance, and somehow the ball rolled into the hole. The next day I read in the story of that high artist of all golf writers, Bernard Darwin, that he'd never before seen a man so nonchalantly hole a 3-foot putt to gain a championship. What a lovely word "nonchalant"—apparently unconcerned, indifferent!

I thanked Mr. Darwin and assured him that from the instant the putter left the ball on the backswing I was blind and unconscious. I was afraid to think about that putt. Everything I could do about it had been done before the putt started. The decision was up to the Fates. If I had putted in my usual style I would have yipped the putt. Maybe it would have holed, maybe not. But before I got to the putt I had decided that I didn't dare gamble. I used what I thought might be near to a fool-proof method to minimize movements of my hands and wavering of the putter head. It worked.

There are cases of the yips hitting in departments other than putting, but they're not so serious or so difficult (or impossible) to cure. There are spells of shanking that are painfully similar to yipping, but the true yip is a short, gentle easy shot that for some terrifying reason is the next stage in punishment after the Chinese water torture.

Zest

est is what golf, and life for that matter, must offer you or it all isn't worth it. When I was a lad in Scotland one of the few beauties of slow play to which we were subjected were church services, and let me tell you that whoever has heard any of the King James version read full of burrs and intensity has heard opera with the angels singing.

There was one line among many that I never will forget and that was Matthew reporting that Jesus asked "For what is a man profited, if he shall gain the whole world and lose his own soul?" With the reverence I was born with and developed, I must say there was a wonderful reminder to figure the odds. I've seen many, includ-

ing some of the famous ones, who haven't been able to
see what the true score is in golf. For what is a man
profited if he sinks a 200-yard approach shot but doesn't
enjoy the game?

I have seen some famous young golfers so sick of the
game that has made them rich they can't stand any more
golf, and have to get away from it for a while to recover
their zest for testing their technique and spirit against
the ball and the course. But I also have seen immensely
successful businessmen who could buy out the first two
dozen wealthiest pro golfers and not bother about the
money, score well over 100 and enjoy a wonderful happy
time. These fellows have the intelligent attitude. And
what a contrast it is to the gloomy expression of the fellow who comes into the locker room with a scorecard
showing a one-under-par 71 and moans, "I 3-putted the
12th and the 15th." Think of that misery, think of what
the sad character missed, not of the score he got.

Maybe I sound like a philosopher broadcasting from
a barrel that faces the sun instead of what I actually am,
a very lucky guy who thoroughly enjoys playing golf
and always will and thanks God for that. I was blessed
by being able to make a living (and spiritually and ma-
terially a very good one, too) in a game that is gloriously
more than a game.

I am grateful that I always have been able to see a
golf course first as scenery, when it actually does appeal
to my sense of the beautiful, and then as golf architecture, which, in some cases makes beautiful use of rather
dull landscape. I find myself thinking of a golf hole as
a picture that continues to please my heart rather than,
primarily, as an arrangement of land calling for a shot

with a slight draw and a quick stop, after a well-placed drive.

I thank heaven I have been able, despite my critical nature, to regard those to whom I've taught (and tried to teach) golf as fellow students, as friends and companion learners, rather than pupils. And I take oath that I have had some unbelievably dumb and inept ones who have been more of a challenge to me than any competitive tournament round ever was. In some cases they have whipped me.

You've missed shots. So have I. So have other mortals. When are we going to realize that missing simple shots is part of being humans? But there are worse things than missing golf shots. I have experienced and recovered from some of these major miseries. When we learn to adjust ourselves to the good and the bad shots, we have learned one of the lessons of golf that is far beyond golf.

Perhaps you won't believe it, but I, who have been a golf workingman for a lot of years, remember more laughs, more pleasant people and more beautiful golf course scenes than I remember wonderful shots I've made. It surprises me to realize that I've become this mellow. To keep on telling the truth, I hope that everybody shares my good fortune in getting to a true sense of values in golf. I am inclined to believe that the British have it over us in soundness of attitude toward golf. They seem to place the fundamental accent on the man and nature, which is elemental golf. We are disposed to think a great deal about the trimmings.

At its highest point in the scheme of things golf simply and sufficiently owes its high status to its value in contributing to the pursuit of happiness. And what a contribution it is for you!

The infinite variety of golf's appeal recently was brought to my mind by a friend who told me that every golf shot he took was a new game. This was a novel, refreshing view of the game. This fellow takes a lot of strokes when he gets away from a very arduous job to renew his mind and body at golf. If he could forget a shot and start all over on another game of golf why should I mourn my mistakes?

Golf actually is more than the shots you take, although that has to be the way the game is scored. We get confused, and aim for the moon when we ought to be content to enjoy the sun. The most delightful, glorious, cheering thing about golf is that it doesn't make sense. And I should know that, for I am credited (and it may be true) with having been paid far more for golf lessons than any other fellow living (or in greener pastures with Young and Old Tom Morris, et al.), but I am reasonably certain that I have given more free golf lessons to aspiring and apparently adept and determined young men and young women than any other fellow in the profession of golf. And with that tutoring went, at my expense, certain other material benefits. So whether I am robber or Robin Hood, the jury will have to decide and, confidentially, I don't give a damn, so long as this round-up of what I've learned will do you some good.